M000209581

R Data Science Quick Reference

A Pocket Guide to APIs, Libraries, and Packages

Thomas Mailund

Apress®

R Data Science Quick Reference: A Pocket Guide to APIs, Libraries, and Packages

Thomas Mailund
Aarhus, Denmark

ISBN-13 (pbk): 978-1-4842-4893-5   ISBN-13 (electronic): 978-1-4842-4894-2
https://doi.org/10.1007/978-1-4842-4894-2

Copyright © 2019 by Thomas Mailund

This work is subject to copyright. All rights are reserved by the Publisher, whether the whole or part of the material is concerned, specifically the rights of translation, reprinting, reuse of illustrations, recitation, broadcasting, reproduction on microfilms or in any other physical way, and transmission or information storage and retrieval, electronic adaptation, computer software, or by similar or dissimilar methodology now known or hereafter developed.

Trademarked names, logos, and images may appear in this book. Rather than use a trademark symbol with every occurrence of a trademarked name, logo, or image we use the names, logos, and images only in an editorial fashion and to the benefit of the trademark owner, with no intention of infringement of the trademark.

The use in this publication of trade names, trademarks, service marks, and similar terms, even if they are not identified as such, is not to be taken as an expression of opinion as to whether or not they are subject to proprietary rights.

While the advice and information in this book are believed to be true and accurate at the date of publication, neither the authors nor the editors nor the publisher can accept any legal responsibility for any errors or omissions that may be made. The publisher makes no warranty, express or implied, with respect to the material contained herein.

Managing Director, Apress Media LLC: Welmoed Spahr
Acquisitions Editor: Steve Anglin
Development Editor: Matthew Moodie
Coordinating Editor: Mark Powers

Cover designed by eStudioCalamar

Cover image designed by Freepik (www.freepik.com)

Distributed to the book trade worldwide by Springer Science+Business Media New York, 233 Spring Street, 6th Floor, New York, NY 10013. Phone 1-800-SPRINGER, fax (201) 348-4505, e-mail orders-ny@springer-sbm.com, or visit www.springeronline.com. Apress Media, LLC is a California LLC and the sole member (owner) is Springer Science + Business Media Finance Inc (SSBM Finance Inc). SSBM Finance Inc is a **Delaware** corporation.

For information on translations, please e-mail editorial@apress.com; for reprint, paperback, or audio rights, please email bookpermissions@springernature.com.

Apress titles may be purchased in bulk for academic, corporate, or promotional use. eBook versions and licenses are also available for most titles. For more information, reference our Print and eBook Bulk Sales web page at http://www.apress.com/bulk-sales.

Any source code or other supplementary material referenced by the author in this book is available to readers on GitHub via the book's product page, located at www.apress.com/9781484248935. For more detailed information, please visit http://www.apress.com/source-code.

Printed on acid-free paper

Table of Contents

About the Author

Thomas Mailund is an associate professor in bioinformatics at Aarhus University, Denmark. He has a background in math and computer science. For the past decade, his main focus has been on genetics and evolutionary studies, particularly comparative genomics, speciation, and gene flow between emerging species. He has published *The Joys of Hashing*, *Domain-Specific Languages in R*, *Beginning Data Science in R*, *Functional Programming in R*, and *Metaprogramming in R*, all from Apress, as well as other books.

About the Technical Reviewer

Dwight Barry is a principal data scientist at Seattle Children's Hospital in Seattle, WA, USA. He's worked in analytics for more than 20 years, in both academia and industry, in the fields of health care, hospital administration, clinical and hospital care, environmental science, and emergency management.

CHAPTER 1

Introduction

R is a functional programming language with a focus on statistical analysis. It has built-in support for model specifications that can be manipulated as first-class objects, and an extensive collection of functions for dealing with probability distributions and model fitting, both built-in and through extension packages.

The language has a long history. It was created in 1992 and is based on an even older language, S, from 1976. Many quirks and inconsistencies have entered the language over the years. There are, for example, at least three partly incompatible ways of implementing object orientation, and one of these is based on a naming convention that clashes with some built-in functions. It can be challenging to navigate through the many quirks of R, but this is alleviated by a suite of extensions, collectively known as the "Tidyverse."

While there are many data science applications that involve more complex data structures, such as graphs and trees, most bread-and-butter analyses involve rectangular data. That is, the analysis is of data that can be structured as a table of rows and columns where, usually, the rows correspond to observations and the columns correspond to explanatory variables and observations. The usual data sets are also of a size that can be loaded into memory and analyzed on a single desktop or laptop. I will assume that both are the case here. If this is not the case, then you need different, big data techniques that go beyond the scope of this book.

The Tidyverse is a collection of extensions to R; packages that are primarily aimed at analyzing tabular data that fits into your computer's

© Thomas Mailund 2019
T. Mailund, *R Data Science Quick Reference*, https://doi.org/10.1007/978-1-4842-4894-2_1

memory. Some of the packages go beyond this, but since data science is predominately manipulation of tabular data, this is the focus of this book.

The Tidyverse packages provide consistent naming conventions, consistent programming interfaces, and more importantly a consistent notation that captures how data analysis consists of different steps of data manipulation and model fitting.

The packages do not merely provide collections of functions for manipulating data but rather small domain-specific languages for different aspects of your analysis. Almost all of these small languages are based on the same overall "pipeline" syntax, so once you know one of them, you can easily use the others. A noticeable exception is the plotting library ggplot2. It is slightly older than the other extensions and because of this has a different syntax. The main difference is the operator used for combining different operations. The data pipeline notation uses the %>% operator, while ggplot2 combines plotting instructions using +. If you are like me, then you will often try to combine ggplot2 instructions using %>%—only out of habit—but once you get an error from R, you will recognize your mistake and can quickly fix it.

This book is a syntax reference for modern data science in R, which means that it is a guide for using Tidyverse packages and it is a guide for programmers who want to use R's Tidyverse packages instead of basic R programming.

This guide does not explain each Tidyverse package exhaustively. The development of Tidyverse packages progresses rapidly, and the book would not contain a complete guide shortly after it is printed anyway. The structure of the extensions and the domain-specific languages they provide are stable, however, and from examples with a subset of the functionality in them, you should not have any difficulties with reading the package documentation for each of them and find the features you need that are not covered in the book.

To get started with the Tidyverse, install and load it:

```
install.packages("tidyverse")
library(tidyverse)
```

The Tidyverse consists of many packages that you can install and load independently, but loading all through the tidyverse package is the easiest, so unless you have good reasons to, just load tidyverse when you start an analysis. In this book I describe three packages that are not loaded from tidyverse but are generally considered part of the Tidyverse.[1]

---

[1]The Tidyverse I refer to here is the ecosystem of Tidyverse packages but not the *package* tidyverse that only loads the key packages.

CHAPTER 2

Importing Data: readr

Before we can analyze data, we need to load it into R. The main Tidyverse package for this is called readr, and it is loaded when you load the tidyverse package.

library(tidyverse)

But you can also load it explicitly using

library(readr)

Tabular data is usually stored in text files or compressed text files with rows and columns matching the table's structure. Each line in the file is a row in the table and columns are separated by a known delimiter character. The readr package is made for such data representation and contains functions for reading and writing variations of files formatted in this way. It also provides functionality for determining the types of data in each column, either by inferring types or through user specifications.

© Thomas Mailund 2019

T. Mailund, *R Data Science Quick Reference*, https://doi.org/10.1007/978-1-4842-4894-2_2

Functions for Reading Data

The readr package provides the following functions for reading tabular data:

Function	File format
read_csv()	Comma-separated values
read_csv2()	Semicolon-separated values
read_tsv()	Tab-separated values
read_delim()	General column delimiters[1]
read_table()	Space-separated values (fixed length columns)
read_table2()	Space-separated values (variable length columns)

The interface to these functions differs little. In the following file, I describe read_csv, but I highlight when the other functions differ. The read_csv function reads data from a file with comma-separated values. Such a file could look like this:

```
A,B,C,D
1,a,a,1.2
2,b,b,2.1
3,c,c,13.0
```

Unlike the base R read.csv function, read_csv will also handle files with spaces between the columns, so it will interpret the following data the same as the preceding file.

---

[1]The read_delim() can handle any file format that has a special character that delimits columns. The read_csv(), read_csv2(), and read_tsv() functions are specializations of it. The first of these uses commas for the delimiter, the second semicolons, and the third tabs.

```
A, B, C,   D
1, a, a,   1.2
2, b, b,   2.1
3, c, c,  13.0
```

If you use R's read.csv function instead, the spaces before columns B and C will be included as part of the data, and the text columns will be interpreted as factors.

The first line in the file will be interpreted as a header, naming the columns, and the remaining three lines as data rows.

Assuming the file is named data/data.csv, you read its data like this:

```
my_data <- read_csv(file = "data/data.csv")

## Parsed with column specification:
## cols(
##   A = col_double(),
##   B = col_character(),
##   C = col_character(),
##   D = col_double()
## )
```

When reading the file, read_csv will infer that columns A and D are numbers and columns B and C are strings.

If the file contains tab-separated values

```
A   B   C   D
1   a   a   1.2
2   b   b   2.1
3   c   c   13.0
```

you should use read_tsv() instead.

```
my_data <- read_tsv(file = "data/data.tsv")
```

The file you read with read_csv can be compressed. If the suffix of the filename is .gz, .bz2, .xz, or .zip, it will be uncompressed before read_csv loads the data.

```
my_data <- read_csv(file = "data/data.csv.gz")
```

If the filename is a URL (i.e., has prefix http://, https://, ftp://, or ftps://), the file will automatically be downloaded.

You can also provide a string as the file object:

```
read_csv(
    "A, B, C,    D
     1, a, a,   1.2
     2, b, b,   2.1
     3, c, c,  13.0
")
```

This is rarely useful in a data analysis project, but you can use it to create examples or for debugging.

File Headers

The first line in a comma-separated file is not always the column names; that information might be available from elsewhere outside the file. If you do not want to interpret the first line as column names, you can use the option col_names = FALSE.

```
read_csv(
    file = "data/data.csv",
    col_names =FALSE
)
```

Since the data/data.csv file *has* a header, that is interpreted as part of the data, and because the header consists of strings, read_csv infers that all the column types are strings. If we did not have the header, for example, if we had the file data/data-no-header.csv:

```
1, a, a, 1.2
2, b, b, 2.1
3, c, c, 13.0
```

then we would get the same data frame as before, except that the names would be autogenerated:

```
read_csv(
    file = "data/data-no-header.csv",
    col_names =FALSE
)

## Parsed with column specification:
## cols(
##     X1 = col_double(),
##     X2 = col_character(),
##     X3 = col_character(),
##     X4 = col_double()
## )

## # A tibble: 3 x 4
##        X1 X2    X3        X4
##     <dbl> <chr> <chr> <dbl>
## 1       1 a     a        1.2
## 2       2 b     b        2.1
## 3       3 c     c       13
```

The autogenerated column names all start with X and are followed by the number the columns have from left to right in the file.

If you have data in a file without a header, but you do not want the autogenerated names, you can provide column names to the col_names option:

```
read_csv(
    file = "data/data-no-header.csv",
    col_names = c("X", "Y", "Z", "W")
)
```

If there is a header line, but you want to rename the columns, you cannot just provide the names to read_csv using col_names. The first row will still be interpreted as data. This gives you data you do not want in the first row, and it also affects the inferred types of the columns.

You can, however, skip lines before read_csv parse rows as data. Since we have a header line in data/data.csv, we can skip one line and set the column names.

```
read_csv(
    file = "data/data.csv",
    col_names = c("X", "Y", "Z", "W"),
    skip = 1
)
```

You can also put a limit on how many data rows you want to load using the n_max option.

```
read_csv(
    file = "data/data.csv",
    col_names = c("X", "Y", "Z", "W"),
    skip = 1,
    n_max = 2
)
```

If your input file has comment lines, identifiable by a character where the rest of the line should be considered a comment, you can skip them if you provide the comment option:

read_csv(
```
  "A, B, C,    D
  # this is a comment
  1, a, a,  1.2 # another comment
  2, b, b,  2.1
  3, c, c, 13.0",
  comment = "#")
```

For more options affecting how input files are interpreted, read the function documentation: ?read_csv.

Column Types

When read_csv parses a file, it infers the type of each column. This inference can be slow, or worse the inference can be incorrect. If you know a priori what the types should be, you can specify this using the col_types option. If you do this, then read_csv will not make a guess at the types. It will, however, replace values that it cannot parse as of the right type into NA.[2]

---

[2]There is a gotcha here. The types are guessed at after a fixed number of lines are read (by default 1000). If you have 1000 lines of numbers in a column and line 1001 has a string, then the type will be inferred as numeric and you lose the string. If you know the types, it is always better to tell the functions what they are.

String-based Column Type Specification

In the simplest string specification format, you must provide a string with the same length as you have columns and where each character in the string specifies the type of one column. The characters specifying different types are this:

Character	Type
C	Character
I	Integer
N	Number
D	Double
L	Logical
F	Factor
D	Date
T	Date time
T	Time
?	Guess (default)
_ / -	Skip the column

By default, read_csv guesses, so we could make this explicit using the type specification "????":

```
read_csv(
    file = "data/data.csv",
    col_types = "????"
)
```

The results of the guesses are double for columns A and D and character for columns B and C. If we wanted to make *this* explicit, we could use "dccd".

```
read_csv(
    file = "data/data.csv",
    col_types = "dccd"
)
```

If you want an integer type for column A, you can use `"iccd"`:

```
read_csv(
    file = "data/data.csv",
    col_types = "iccd"
)
```

If you try to interpret column D as integers as well, you will get a list of warning messages, and the values in column D will all be NA; the numbers in column D cannot be interpreted as integers and read_csv will not round them to integers.

If you specify that a column should have type d, the numbers in the column must be integers or decimal numbers. If you use the type n (the default that read_csv will guess), you will also get doubles, but the latter type can handle strings that can be interpreted as numbers such as dollar amounts, percentages, and group separators in numbers. The column type n will ignore leading and trailing text and handle number separators:

With this function call

```
read_csv(
    'A, B, C,  D,         E
    $1, a, a,  1.2%, "1,100,200"
    $2, b, b,  2.1%,   "140,000"
    $3, c, c, 13.0%, "2,005,000"',
    col_types = "nccnn")
```

columns A, D, and E will be read as numbers. If you use the type specification d, they would not, and all the values would be NA.

The decimal indicator and group delimiter vary around the world. By default, read_csv uses the US convention with a dot for decimal notation and comma for grouping in numbers. In many European countries, it is the opposite. You can use the locale option to change these:

read_csv(
```
    'A, B, C,  D,                E
    $1, a, a,  "1,2%",    "1.100.200"
    $2, b, b,  "2,1%",     "140.000"
    $3", c, c, 13,0%",    "2.005.000"',
    locale=locale(decimal_mark = ",",grouping_mark  ="."),
    col_types = "nccnn")
```

In the preceding example, I explicitly specified how read_csv should interpret numbers, but you can also use ISO 639-1 language codes.[3] If you do, you also get the local time conventions and local day and month names. The default is English, but if your data is from Denmark, for example, you want to use Danish conventions, you would use the local locale("da"). For French data, you would use fr, locale("fr"). If you type this into an R console, you will see the month and week names, including their abbreviated forms, in these languages.

See the ?locale documentation for more options.

In files that use commas as decimal points and "." for number groupings, the column delimiter is usually ";" rather than ",". This way, it is not necessary to put decimal numbers in quotes. The read_csv2 function works as read_csv but uses ";" as column delimiter and "." for number groupings.

---

[3]https://en.wikipedia.org/wiki/List_of_ISO_639-1_codes

The *logical* type is used for boolean values. If a column only contains TRUE and FALSE (case doesn't matter),

read_csv(
```
    'A,   B, C,      D
    TRUE,    a, a,   1.2
    false,   b, b,   2.1
    true,    c, c, 13')
```

then read_csv will guess that the type is logical.

It is not unusual to code boolean values as 0 and 1; however, and since these will be interpreted as numbers by default, you can make their type explicit using l:

read_csv(
```
    'A, B, C,    D
    1, a, a,   1.2
    0, b, b,   2.1
    1, c, c, 13',
    col_types = "lccn")
```

If you use type l, you can mix TRUE/FALSE (ignoring case) with 0/1. Any other number or string will be translated into NA.

The D, t, and T types are for *dates*, *time points*, and *datetime*, in that order. Dates and time are what you might expect. A date specifies a range of days, for example, a single day, a week, a month, or a year. A time points a specific time of the day, for example, an hour, a minute, or a second. A datetime combines a day and a time, that is, it specifies a specific time during a specific day.

read_csv(
```
    'D, T, t
    "2018-08-23", "2018-08-23T14:30",   14:30',
    col_types = "DTt"
)
```

```
## # A tibble: 1 x 3
##   D           T                   t
##   <date>      <dttm>              <drtn>
## 1 2018-08-23 2018-08-23 14:30:00 14:30
```

If you use one of these type specifications, the time and dates should be in ISO 8601 format.[4] Local conventions for writing time and date, however, differ substantially and are rarely ISO 8601. When your time data are not ISO 8601, you need to tell read_csv how to read them.

The default time parser handles times in the hh:mm, hh:mm:ss formats and handles am and pm suffixes; it suffices for most time formats (but notice that it wants time in hh:mm or hh:mm:ss formats; it is flexible in the number of characters you use for hours, and you can leave out seconds, but you cannot leave out minutes). Date and datetime vary much more than time formats, and there, you usually need to specify the encoding format.

You can use the locale option to change how read_csv parses dates (D) and time (t).

```
read_csv(
    'D,  t
    "23 Oct 2018",  pm',
    col_types = "Dt",
    locale = locale(
        date_format = "%d %b %Y",
        time_format = "%I%p"
    )
)
```

The date_format "%d %b %Y" says that dates are written as day, three-letter month abbreviation, and year with four digits, and each of the three separated by a space. The time_format "%I%p" says that we want

---

[4]https://en.wikipedia.org/wiki/ISO_8601

time to be written as a number from 1 to 12, with no minute information, the hour immediately followed by am/pm without any space between.

For data times (T), we cannot specify the format using `locale`. We need a more verbose type specification that we return to the following specification. We also return to formatting specifications for parsing dates and time later.

Columns that are not immediately parsed as numbers, booleans, dates, or times will be parsed as *strings*. If you want these to be factors instead, you use the f type specification.

read_csv(
```
    'A, B, C,     D
    1, a, a,   1.2
    0, b, b,   2.1
    1, c, c,  13',
    col_types = "lcfn")

    ## # A tibble: 3 x 4
    ##     A      B      C      D
    ##   <lgl>  <chr>  <fct>  <dbl>
    ## 1 TRUE   a      a        1.2
    ## 2 FALSE  b      b        2.1
    ## 3 TRUE   c      c       13
```

If you only want to use some of the columns, you can skip the rest using the "type" - or _:

read_csv(
```
    file = "data/data.csv",
    col_type = "_cc-"
)

## # A tibble: 3 x 2
##     B      C
```

```
##    <chr> <chr>
## 1 a     a
## 2 b     b
## 3 c     c
```

If you specify the column types using a string, you should specify the types of all columns. If you only want to define the types of a subset of columns, you can use the function cols() to specify types. You call this function with named parameters, where the names are column names and the arguments are types.

```
read_csv(
    file = "data/data.csv",
    col_types = cols(A = "c")
)
read_csv(
    file = "data/data.csv",
    col_types = cols(A = "c", D = "c")
)
```

Function-based Column Type Specification

If you are like me, you might find it hard to remember the single-character codes for different types. If so, you can use longer type names that you specify using function calls. These functions have names that start with col_, so you can use autocomplete to get a list of them. The types you can specify using functions are the same as those you can specify using characters, of course, and the functions are:

Function	Type
col_character()	Character
col_integer()	Integer
col_number()	Number
col_double()	Double
col_logical()	Logical
col_factor()	Factor
col_date()	Date
col_datetime()	Date time
col_time()	Time
col_guess()	Guess (default)
col_skip()	Skip the column

You need to wrap the function-based type specifications in a call to cols.

```
read_csv(
    file = "data/data.csv",
    col_types = cols(A = col_integer())
)

## # A tibble: 3 x 4
##      A B     C          D
##   <int> <chr> <chr>  <dbl>
## 1     1 a     a        1.2
## 2     2 b     b        2.1
## 3     3 c     c         13

read_csv(
    file = "data/data.csv",
    col_types = cols(D = col_character())
)
```

```
## # A tibble: 3 x 4
##        A B     C     D
##    <dbl> <chr> <chr> <chr>
## 1     1 a     a     1.2
## 2     2 b     b     2.1
## 3     3 c     c     13.0
```

Most of the col_ functions do not take any arguments, but they are affected by the locale parameter the same way that the string specifications are.

For factors, date, time, and datetime types, however, you have more control over the format using the col_ functions. You can use arguments to these functions for specifying how read_csv should parse dates and how it should construct factors.

For factors, you can explicitly set the levels. If you do not, then the column parser will set the levels in the order it sees the different strings in the column. For example, in data/data.csv the strings in columns C and D are in the order a, b, and c:

```
A, B, C,   D
1, a, a,   1.2
2, b, b,   2.1
3, c, c, 13.0
```

By defaults, the two columns will be interpreted as characters, but if we specify that C should be a factor, we get one where the levels are a, b, and c, in that order.

```
my_data <- read_csv(
    file = "data/data.csv",
    col_types = cols(C = col_factor())
)
```

```
my_data$C
```

```
## [1] a b c
## Levels: a b c
```

If we want the levels in a different order, we can give col_factor() a levels argument.

```
my_data <- read_csv(
    file = "data/data.csv",
    col_types = cols(
        C = col_factor(levels = c("c", "b", "a"))
    )
)
my_data$C
```

```
## [1] a b c
## Levels: c b a
```

We can also make factors ordered using the ordered argument.

```
my_data <- read_csv(
    file = "data/data.csv",
    col_types = cols(
        B = col_factor(ordered = TRUE),
        C = col_factor(levels = c("c", "b", "a"))
    )
)
my_data$B
```

```
## [1] a b c
## Levels: a < b < c
```

```
my_data$C
```

```
## [1] a b c
## Levels: c b a
```

Parsing Time and Dates

The most complex types to read (or write) are dates *and* time (and datetime), just because these are written in many different ways. You can specify the format that dates and datetime are in using a string with codes that indicate how time information is represented.

The codes are these:

Code	Time format	Example string	Interpretation
%Y	4-digit year	1975	The year 1975
%y	2-digit year[5]	75	Also the year 75
%m	2-digit month	02	February
%b	Abbreviated month name[6]	Feb	February
%B	Full month name	February	February
%d	2-digit day	15	The 15th of a month
%H	Hour number on a 24-hour clock	18	Six o'clock in the evening
%I	Hour number on a 12-hour clock[7]	6 pm	18:00 hours
%p	AM/PM indicator	6 pm	18:00 hours

---

[5]Two-digit years are assumed to be either in the twentieth or the twenty-first century. The cutoff line is 68; years at or below 68 are in the twentieth century and 69 and above are in the twenty-first century. Therefore, 75 is assumed to be in the twentieth century, so 75 is 1975.

[6]The name of months and weekdays varies from language to language, and so does the abbreviations. Therefore, if you use a format that refers to these, you either need to use numbers or the format will depend on the locale option.

[7]If you use %I, you must also use %p for pm/am.

Code	Time format	Example string	Interpretation
%M	Two-digit minutes	18:30	Half past six
%S	Integer seconds	18:30:10	Ten seconds past 18:00
%Z	Time zone as name[8]	America/Chicago	Central Time
%z	Time zone as o_set from UTC	"+0100"	Central European Time

There are shortcuts for frequently used formats:

Shortcut	Format
%D	%m/%d/%y
%x	%y/%m/%d
%F	%Y-%m-%d
%R	%H:%M
%T	%H:%M:%S

As we saw earlier, you can set the date and time format using the locale() function. If you do not, the default codes will be %AD for dates and %AT for time (there is no locale() argument for datetime). These codes specify YMD and H:M/H:M:S formats, respectively, but are more relaxed in matching the patterns. The date parse, for example, will allow different separators. For dates, both "1975-02-15" and "1975/02/15" will be read as February the 15th 1975, and for time, both "18:00" and "6:00 pm" will be six o'clock in the evening.

---

[8]Time zones based on locations handle daylight saving time. UTC is a fixed time zone, and it does not have daylight saving time.

In the following text, I give a few examples. I will use the functions parse_date, parse_time, and parse_datetime rather than read_csv with column type specifications. These functions are used by read_csv when you specify a date, time, or datetime column type, but using read_csv for the examples would be unnecessarily verbose. Each takes a vector string representation of dates and time. For more examples, you can read the function documentation ?col_datetime.

Parsing time is simplest; there is not much variation in how time points are written. The main differences are in whether you use 24-hour clocks or 12-hour clocks. The %R and %T codes expect 24-hour clocks and differ in whether seconds are included or not.

```
parse_time(c("18:00"), format = "%R")
parse_time(c("18:00:30"), format = "%T")
```

There is no shortcut for 12-hour codes, but you must combine %I with %p to read PM/AM formats.

```
parse_time(c("6 pm"), format = "%I %p")
```

Here, I have specified that the input only includes hours and not minutes. If we want hours (and not minutes) in 24-hour clocks, we need to use %H rather than %R.

For dates, ISO 8601 says that the format should be YYYY-MM-DD. The default date parser will accept this format, but the explicit format string is

```
parse_date(c("1975/02/05"), format = "%Y/%m/%d")
```

If you do not want to include the day, and you want to use two-digit years, you need

```
parse_date(c("75-02"), format = "%y-%m")
```

This is February 1975; remember that the %y code assumes that numbers above 68 are in the twentieth century.

Dates written on the form 05/02/75 can mean both February 15th 1975 and May 2nd 1975, depending on where you are in the world. Europe uses the sensible DD/MM/YY format, where the order goes from the smallest time unit, days, to the medium time units, months, and then to years. In the United States, they use the MM/DD/YY format. To get the 15th of February, you need one of these formats:

```
parse_date(c("75/02/05"), format = "%y/%m/%d")
parse_date(c("75/05/02"), format = "%y/%d/%m")
```

Date specifications that only use numbers are not affected by the local language, but if you include the name of months, they are. The name of months and their abbreviation varies from language to language, obviously. So do the name of weekdays, but at the time of writing, parsing weeks and weekdays is not supported by readr. You can get the name information from locale() if you use a language code. In the following examples, I parse dates in English and Danish. The month names are almost the same, but abbreviations in Danish require a dot following them, and the day is followed by a dot as well.

```
parse_date(c("Feb 15 1975"),
           format = "%b %d %Y", locale = locale("en"))
parse_date(c("15. feb. 1975"),
           format = "%d. %b %Y", locale = locale("da"))
parse_date(c("February 15 1975"),
           format = "%B %d %Y", locale = locale("en"))
parse_date(c("15. feb. 1975"),
           format = "%d. %b %Y", locale = locale("da"))

parse_date(c("Oct 15 1975"),
           format = "%b %d %Y", locale = locale("en"))
parse_date(c("15. okt. 1975"),
           format = "%d. %b %Y", locale = locale("da"))
```

```
parse_date(c("October 15 1975"),
           format = "%B %d %Y", locale = locale("en"))
parse_date(c("15. oktober 1975"),
           format = "%d. %B %Y", locale = locale("da"))
```

Datetimes can be parsed using combinations of date and time strings. With these, you also want to consider time zones. You can ignore those for dates and time, but unless you are sure that you will never have to consider time zones, you should not rely on the default time zone (which is UTC).[9]

You can either specify that time zones are relative to UTC with %z or location-based, with %Z if the time zone is given in the input, or you can use locale() if it is the same for all the input.

If you specify a time zone based on a location, R will automatically adjust for daylight saving time, but if you use dates relative to UTC, you will not—UTC does not have daylight savings. Central European Time (CET) is "+0100" and with daylight saving time "+0200". US Pacific Time is "-0800", but with daylight saving time, it is "-0900". When you switch back and forth between daylight savings is determined by your location.

These two datetimes are the same

```
parse_datetime(c("Feb 15 1975 18:00 US/Pacific"),
               format = "%b %d %Y %R %Z")
parse_datetime(c("Feb 15 1975 18:00 -0800"),
               format = "%b %d %Y %R %z")
```

as are these two

```
parse_datetime(c("May 15 1975 18:00 US/Pacific"),
               format = "%b %d %Y %R %Z")
parse_datetime(c("May 15 1975 18:00 -0900"),
               format = "%b %d %Y %R %z")
```

---

[9]https://en.wikipedia.org/wiki/Coordinated_Universal_Time

If you use locale() to specify a time zone, you cannot use zones relative to UTC. The point of using locale() is local formats, not time zones. The parser will still handle daylight savings for you, however. These two are the same datetimes

```
parse_datetime(c("Aug 15 1975 18:00"),
               format = "%b %d %Y %R",
               locale = locale(tz = "US/Pacific"))
parse_datetime(c("Aug 15 1975 18:00 US/Pacific"),
               format = "%b %d %Y %R %Z")
```

If you print the objects you parse, there is a difference between using locale() and using %Z, but the time will be the same. Using %Z you will automatically translate the time into UTC; using locale() you will not.

```
x <- parse_datetime(c("Aug 15 1975 18:00"),
                    format = "%b %d %Y %R",
                    locale = locale(tz = "US/Pacific"))
x
```

```
## [1] "1975-08-15 18:00:00 PDT"
```

```
y <- parse_datetime(c("Aug 15 1975 18:00 US/Pacific"),
                    format = "%b %d %Y %R %Z")
y
```

```
## [1] "1975-08-16 01:00:00 UTC"
```

```
x == y
```

```
## [1] TRUE
```

The output looks like a string, but the object classes are not character, which, among other things, is why the comparison works.

Space-separated Columns

The preceding functions all read delimiter-separated columns. They expect a single character to separate one column from the next. If the argument `trim_ws` is true, they ignore whitespace. This argument is true by default for `read_csv`, `read_csv2`, and `read_tsv`, but false for `read_delim`.

The functions `read_table` and `read_table2` take a different approach and separate columns by one or more spaces. The simplest of the two is `read_table2`. It expects any sequence of whitespace to separate columns. Consider

```
read_table2(
    "A B C D
     1 2 3 4
     15 16 17 18"
)

## # A tibble: 2 x 4
##       A     B     C     D
##   <dbl> <dbl> <dbl> <dbl>
## 1     1     2     3     4
## 2    15    16    17    18
```

The header names are separated by two spaces. The first data line has spaces before the first line since the string is indented the way it is. Between columns, there are also two spaces. For the second data line, we have several spaces before the first value, once again, but this time only single space between the columns. If we used a delimiter character to specify that we wanted a space to separate columns, we had to have exactly the same number of spaces between each column.

The `read_table` function instead reads the data as fixed-width columns. It uses the whitespace in the file to figure out the width of the columns. After this, each line will be split into characters that match the width of the columns and assigned to those columns.

For example, in

read_table(
```
"
    A       B       C   D
    121     xyz     14  15
    22      abc     24  25
"
)
```

```
## # A tibble: 2 x 4
##       A B           C     D
##    <dbl> <chr>   <dbl> <dbl>
## 1   121 xyz        14    15
## 2    22 abc        24    25
```

the columns are aligned, and the rows are interpreted as we might expect. Aligned, here, means that we have aligned spaces at some position between the columns. If you do not have spaces at the same location in all rows, columns will be merged.

read_table(
```
"
    A   B    C D
    121 xyz 14 15
    22  abc 24 25
"
)
```

```
## # A tibble: 2 x 3
##         A B      `C D`
##     <dbl> <chr> <chr>
## 1     121 xyz     14 15
## 2      22 abc     24 25
```

Here, the header C is at the position that should separate columns C and D, and these columns are therefore merged.

If you have spaces in all rows but data between them in some columns only, you will get an error. For example, if your data looks like this

read_table(
```
    "
    A     B    C D
   121    xyz x 14 15
    22    abc    24 25
    "
)
```

where the x in the first data line sits between two all-space columns. If you need more specialized fixed-width files, you might want to consider the read_fwf function. See its documentation for details: ?read_fwf.

The read_table and read_table2 functions take many of the same arguments as the delimiter-based parser, so you can, for example, specify column types and set the locale in the same way as the preceding data.

Not part of the main Tidyverse, the packages loaded when you load the package tidyverse, is readxl. Its read_excel function does exactly what it says on the tin; it reads Excel spreadsheets into R. Its interface is similar to the functions in readr. Where the interface differs is in Excel specific options such as which sheet to read. Such options are clearly only needed when reading Excel files.

Functions for Writing Data

Writing data to a file is more straightforward than reading data because we have the data in the correct types and we do not need to deal with different formats. With readr's writing functions, we have fewer options to format our output—for example, we cannot give the functions a locale() and we cannot specify date and time formatting, but we can use different functions to specify delimiters and time will be output in ISO 8601 which is what the reading functions will use as default.

The functions are write_delim(), write_csv(), write_csv2(), and write_tsv(), and for formats that Excel can read, write_excel_csv() and write_excel_csv2(). The difference between write_csv() and write_excel_csv() and between write_csv2() and write_excel_csv2() is that the Excel functions include a UTF-8 byte order mark so Excel knows that the file is UTF-8 encoded.

The first argument to these functions is the data we want to write and the second is the path to the file we want to write to. If this file has suffix .gz, .bz2, or .xz, the output is automatically compressed.

I will not list all the arguments for these functions here, but you can read the documentation for them from the R console. The argument you are most likely to use is col_names which, if true, means that the function will write the column names as the first line in the output, and if false, will not. If you use write_delim(), you might also want to specify the delimiter character using the delim argument. By default it is a single space; if you write to a file using write_delim() with the default options, you get the data in a format that you can read using read_table2().

The delimiter characters and the decimal points for write_csv(), write_csv2(), and write_tsv are the same as for the corresponding read functions.

CHAPTER 3

Representing Tables: tibble

The data that the readr package returns are represented as tibble objects. These are tabular data representations similar to the base R data frames but are a more modern version.

The package that implements tibbles is tibble. You can load it using:

library(tibble)

Or as part of the tidy verse:

library(tidyverse)

Creating Tibbles

Tidyverse functions that create tabular data will create tibbles rather than data frames. For example, when we use read_csv to read a file into memory, the result is a tibble:

```
x <- read_csv(file = "data/data.csv")

## Parsed with column specification:
## cols(
##   A = col_double(),
##   B = col_character(),
```

```
##   C = col_character(),
##   D = col_double()
## )
```

```
x
```

```
## # A tibble: 3 x 4
##      A  B     C     D
##   <dbl> <chr> <chr> <dbl>
## 1    1  a     a     1.2
## 2    2  b     b     2.1
## 3    3  c     c     13
```

The table that read_csv() creates has several super-classes, but the last is data.frame.

class(x)

```
## [1] "spec_tbl_df" "tbl_df" "tbl"
## [4] "data.frame"
```

This means that generic functions, if not specialized in the other classes, will use the data.frame version, and this, in turn, means that you can often use tibbles in functions that expect data frames. It does not mean that you can *always* use tibbles as a replacement for a data frame. If you run into this problem, you can translate a tibble into a data frame using as.data.frame():

y <- **as.data.frame**(x)
y

```
##   A B C    D
## 1 1 a a  1.2
## 2 2 b b  2.1
## 3 3 c c 13.0
```

```
class(y)
```

```
## [1] "data.frame"
```

Notice that the two objects, when printed, give different output. When printing a tibble, there is more information about the column types.

If you have a data frame, you can translate it into a tibble using as_tibble():

```
z <- as_tibble(y)
z
```

```
## # A tibble: 3 x 4
##       A B     C          D
##    <dbl> <chr> <chr> <dbl>
## 1     1 a     a       1.2
## 2     2 b     b       2.1
## 3     3 c     c        13
```

You can create a tibble from vectors using the tibble() function:

```
x <- tibble(
    x = 1:100,
    y = x^2,
    z = y^2
)
x
```

```
## # A tibble: 100 x 3
##        x     y     z
##    <int> <dbl> <dbl>
## 1     1     1     1
## 2     2     4    16
## 3     3     9    81
## 4     4    16   256
## 5     5    25   625
```

```
##  6       6     36   1296
##  7       7     49   2401
##  8       8     64   4096
##  9       9     81   6561
## 10      10    100  10000
## # ... with 90 more rows
```

Two things to notice here: when you print a tibble, you only see the first ten lines. This is because the tibble has enough lines that it will flood the console if you print all of them. If a tibble has more than 20 rows, you will only see the first ten. If it has fewer, you will see all the rows.

You can change how many lines you will see using the n option to print():

print(x, n = 2)

```
## # A tibble: 100 x 3
##       x     y     z
##   <int> <dbl> <dbl>
## 1     1     1     1
## 2     2     4    16
## # ... with 98 more rows
```

If a tibble has more columns than your console can show, only some will be printed. You can change the number of characters it will print using the width option to print.

print(x, n = 2, width = 15)

```
## # A tibble:
## #   100 x 3
##       x     y
##   <int> <dbl>
## 1     1     1
## 2     2     4
```

```
## # ... with 98
## #   more rows,
## #   and 1 more
## #   variable:
## #   z <dbl>
```

You can set either option to Inf. If n is Inf, you will see all rows, and if width is Inf, you will see all the columns.

The second thing to notice is that you can refer to previous columns when specifying later columns. When we created x, we used

```
tibble(
    x = 1:100,
    y = x^2,
    z = y^2
)
```

where column y refers to column x and column z refers to column y. You cannot refer to variable in the following columns, so this would be an error:

```
tibble(
    w = x/2,
    x = 1:100
)
```

When you use tibble() to create a data frame, you specify the columns as named arguments. If you indent your code as I have in the above example, then you can think of this as defining each column in one line. You can also create a tibble with one line per row.

```
tribble(
    ~x, ~y,  ~z,
    1, 10, 100,
```

```
    2, 20, 200,
    3, 30, 300
)

## # A tibble: 3 x 3
##       x     y     z
##    <dbl> <dbl> <dbl>
## 1     1    10   100
## 2     2    20   200
## 3     3    30   300
```

The first line names the columns, and the ~ is necessary before the names. For large tibbles, using `tribble()` is not that helpful, but for example code or small tables, it can be.

Indexing Tibbles

You can index a tibble in much the same way as you can index a data frame. You can extract a column using single-bracket index ([ ]), either by name or by index:

```
x <- read_csv(file = "data/data.csv")

## Parsed with column specification:
## cols(
##    A = col_double(),
##    B = col_character(),
##    C = col_character(),
##    D = col_double()
## )

y <- as.data.frame(x)
x["A"]
```

```
## # A tibble: 3 x 1
##       A
##   <dbl>
## 1     1
## 2     2
## 3     3
```

```
y["A"]
```

```
##   A
## 1 1
## 2 2
## 3 3
```

```
x[1]
```

```
## # A tibble: 3 x 1
##       A
##   <dbl>
## 1     1
## 2     2
## 3     3
```

```
y[1]
```

```
##   A
## 1 1
## 2 2
## 3 3
```

The result is a tibble or data.frame, respectively, containing a single column.

If you use double brackets ([[ ]]), you will get the vector contained in a column rather than a tibble/data frame:

```
x[["A"]]
```

```
## [1] 1 2 3
```

```
y[["A"]]
```

```
## [1] 1 2 3
```

You will also get the underlying vector of a column if you use $-indexing:

```
x$A
```

```
## [1] 1 2 3
```

```
y$A
```

```
## [1] 1 2 3
```

Using [ ] you can extract more than one column.

```
x[c("A", "C")]
```

```
## # A tibble: 3 x 2
##       A C
##    <dbl> <chr>
## 1     1 a
## 2     2 b
## 3     3 c
```

```
y[c("A", "C")]
```

```
##   A C
## 1 1 a
```

```
## 2 2 b
## 3 3 c
```

```
x[1:2]
```

```
## # A tibble: 3 x 2
##        A B
##    <dbl> <chr>
## 1     1 a
## 2     2 b
## 3     3 c
```

```
y[1:2]
```

```
##    A B
## 1 1 a
## 2 2 b
## 3 3 c
```

You cannot do this using [[ ]].

You can extract a subset of rows and columns if you use two indices. For example, you can get the first two rows in the first two columns using [1:2,1:2]:

```
x[1:2,1:2]
```

```
## # A tibble: 2 x 2
##        A B
##    <dbl> <chr>
## 1     1 a
## 2     2 b
```

```
y[1:2,1:2]
```

```
##    A B
## 1 1 a
## 2 2 b
```

With a single index, you always extract a subset of columns. If you want to extract a subset of rows for all columns, you can use

```
x[1:2,]
```

```
## # A tibble: 2 x 4
##       A B     C       D
##   <dbl> <chr> <chr> <dbl>
## 1     1 a     a       1.2
## 2     2 b     b       2.1
```

```
y[1:2,]
```

```
##   A B C   D
## 1 1 a a 1.2
## 2 2 b b 2.1
```

If you extract a subset of rows from a single column, tibbles and data frames no longer have the same behavior. A tibble will give you a tibble in return, while a data frame will give you a vector:

```
x[1:2,2]
```

```
## # A tibble: 2 x 1
##   B
##   <chr>
## 1 a
## 2 b
```

```
y[1:2,2]
```

```
## [1] "a" "b"
```

Tibbles are more consistent. When you extract part of a tibble, you always get a tibble in return. Data frames sometimes give you a data frame and sometimes (in this particular case) a vector. In any function that expects a data frame and only use subscripts that return a data frame, you can also use a tibble. Tibbles return tibbles, and since a tibble is also a data frame, this will not cause any problems. If a function expects to extract a vector, you cannot use a tibble. This is where you will need to use as.data. frame() to get a data.frame() with data frame behavior.

CHAPTER 4

Reformatting Tables: tidyr

Even if we only consider tabular data, there are still many different ways to format this data. The packages in the Tidyverse expect that data is represented as so-called "tidy data"[1] (which is where the name Tidyverse comes from). The tidyr package helps you with formatting your data into tidy data.

You can load tidyr as part of the Tidyverse

library(tidyverse)

or on its own

library(tidyr)

Tidy Data

The fundamental properties that characterize tidy data are that each variable is in a column, and each observation is in a row. The terms like variables and observations should be familiar from statistics, but what the tidy data properties say is that you should not put the values of a variable in different columns and you should not put more than one observation in the same row.

---

[1]https://en.wikipedia.org/wiki/Tidy_data

© Thomas Mailund 2019
T. Mailund, *R Data Science Quick Reference*, https://doi.org/10.1007/978-1-4842-4894-2_4

Consider data such as this:

```
mean_income <- tribble(
    ~country,   ~`2001`,   ~`2002`,   ~`2003`,   ~`2004`,   ~`2005`,
    "Numenor",  123456,    132654,    321646,    324156,    325416,
    "Westeros", 314256,    432165,    546123,    465321,    561423,
    "Narnia",   432156,    342165,    564123,    543216,    465321,
    "Gondor",   531426,    321465,    235461,    463521,    561423,
    "Laputa",    14235,     34125,     45123,     51234,     54321
)
```

We could imagine that this table contains the mean income in five
(fictional) countries in the first 5 years of the twenty-first century. Let us
say that you are interested in knowing if there is a pattern in income over
time when taking the different countries into account. To do this, you
might consider a formula such as income ~ country + year, but the data
is not formatted in a way that makes this easy. If year is a variable that you
can use in the model, it is a problem that different observations, the actual
years, are split into different columns. Similarly, if the mean income per
year is a variable, it is a problem that all the observations for a country are
in the same row. You cannot use income ~ country + year because the
data is not tidy.

Gather and Spread

The function gather() can merge several columns into two—a key and a
value column. The key column will be a discrete variable with values taken
from the column names, and the value column will contain the data from
the original columns.

Consider the mean income data frame. We want the actual years to be different outcomes of a year variable and have the income for each year to be another variable, income. We can get such a tibble by calling gather() with these parameters:

```
gather(
    data = mean_income,
    key = "year",
    value = "income",
    `2001`, `2001`, `2002`,
    `2003`, `2004`, `2005`
)
```

```
## # A tibble: 25 x 3
##    country  year  income
##    <chr>    <chr> <dbl>
## 1 Numenor  2001  123456
## 2 Westeros 2001  314256
## 3 Narnia   2001  432156
## 4 Gondor   2001  531426
## 5 Laputa   2001   14235
## 6 Numenor  2002  132654
## 7 Westeros 2002  432165
## 8 Narnia   2002  342165
## 9 Gondor   2002  321465
## 10 Laputa  2002   34125
## # ... with 15 more rows
```

The data argument is the input data, and the key and value arguments are the names of two new columns. In the key column, we get the names of the columns we gather, and in the value column, we get the matching values from those columns. The remaining parameters specify which columns we wish to gather.

In the preceding example, I explicitly listed all the columns to gather. You can also use a range of columns, like this:

```
gather(
    data = mean_income,
    key = "year",
    value = "income",
    `2001`:`2005`
)
```

You can use more than one range:

```
gather(
    data = mean_income,
    key = "year",
    value = "income",
    `2001`:`2002`,
    `2004`:`2005`
)
```

but the range specification is only useful when the relevant columns are contiguous. You can also specify the complement of the columns you want to gather using minus. For example, if you want to gather the years, you can pick all columns except for country rather than pick all the years:

```
gather(
    data = mean_income,
    key = "year",
    value = "income",
    -country
)
```

You can specify more than one column in a complement, and you can combine complements with ranges.

Finally, you can combine gather() with tidy selection (see Chapter 3) to select columns.

```
gather(
    data = mean_income,
    key = "year",
    value = "income",
    tidyselect::starts_with("2")
)
gather(
    data = mean_income,
    key = "year",
    value = "income",
    -tidyselect::starts_with("c")
)
```

The column names that go into the key column will be strings. If they can be translated into logical or numeric values, you can do so by setting the argument convert to TRUE.

```
gather(
    data = mean_income,
    key = "year",
    value = "income",
    -country,
    convert = TRUE
)
## # A tibble: 25 x 3
##    country   year income
##    <chr>    <int>  <dbl>
## 1 Numenor   2001 123456
## 2 Westeros  2001 314256
```

```
##  3 Narnia     2001 432156
##  4 Gondor     2001 531426
##  5 Laputa     2001  14235
##  6 Numenor    2002 132654
##  7 Westeros   2002 432165
##  8 Narnia     2002 342165
##  9 Gondor     2002 321465
## 10 Laputa     2002  34125
## # ...  with 15 more rows
```

Because all the years are integers, the year column now contains integers. If we want to analyze this data set, we most likely want to interpret the years as integers.

If you want to translate strings into factors, you have to do this explicitly after the transformation.

If you work with functions that do not expect tidy data and rather expect to find related data in different columns, you can translate tidy data into that format using the spread() function. It is the reverse of gather().[2]

```
tidy_income <- gather(
    data = mean_income,
    key = "year",
    value = "income",
    -country,
    convert = TRUE
)
```

---

[2]The gather() and spread() functions transform tibbles in opposite directions in the sense that I have described here, but they are not truly each other's reverse. The types of values can change depending on the convert argument to gather(), and the order of rows can change.

```
spread(
    data = tidy_income,
    key = "year",
    value = "income"
)
```

```
## # A tibble: 5 x 6
##    country  `2001` `2002` `2003` `2004` `2005`
##    <chr>     <dbl>  <dbl>  <dbl>  <dbl>  <dbl>
## 1 Gondor   531426 321465 235461 463521 561423
## 2 Laputa    14235  34125  45123  51234  54321
## 3 Narnia   432156 342165 564123 543216 465321
## 4 Numenor  123456 132654 321646 324156 325416
## 5 Westeros 314256 432165 546123 465321 561423
```

The key and value arguments pick the values to use as column names and the values to put in those columns, respectively. They are the same arguments that you would use for gather()'s key and value arguments to translate the result back again.

Complex Column Encodings

Different variables are not always represented in separated columns. For example, it is not uncommon to have a column that contains a date, but that is really a day and a month and possibly a year. The best representation of a date is, of course, a date object, but for the sake of the example, let us say that we want to split a date into a day and a month column. You can do this using the separate() function.

```
tbl <- tribble(
    ~date,
    "11/5",
```

```
    "4/7",
    "21/12"
)
separate(tbl, date, into = c("day", "month"))
```

```
## # A tibble: 3 x 2
##    day   month
##    <chr> <chr>
## 1 11    5
## 2 4     7
## 3 21    12
```

The first argument is the data table, the second the column you want to split, and the into argument is a list of the columns the original date will be put into.

By default, the original column is removed, but if you want to keep it, you can use the remove argument.

```
separate(tbl, date, into = c("day", "month"), remove = FALSE)
```

```
## # A tibble: 3 x 3
##    date  day   month
##    <chr> <chr> <chr>
## 1 11/5  11    5
## 2 4/7   4     7
## 3 21/12 21    12
```

After separating the fields in the data column, which is a column of strings, you get a day and a month column, and these also contain strings. To convert them into numbers, you can use the convert argument.

```
separate(tbl, date, into = c("day", "month"), convert = TRUE)
```

```
## # A tibble: 3 x 2
##     day month
```

```
##    <int> <int>
## 1    11     5
## 2     4     7
## 3    21    12
```

By default a column will be split on any non-alphanumeric character. This is why / in the data is correctly used as the separator between the day and the month. If your separator is something else, you can use the sep argument. The argument takes a regular expression, and the column will be split on this. For example, we can split on alphabet characters and spaces like this:

```
tbl <- tribble(
    ~date,
    "11th of month 5",
    "4th of month 7",
    "21st of month 12"
)
separate(tbl, date, into = c("day", "month"),
         sep = "([:alpha:]|[:space:])+")

## # A tibble: 3 x 2
##    day   month
##    <chr> <chr>
## 1 11     5
## 2 4      7
## 3 21     12
```

The date format in this example is not something you would find in the wild, but if we have the date in this format

```
tbl <- tribble(
    ~date,
    "11th of May",
    "4th of July",
    "21st of December"
)
```

we cannot easily distinguish the separator string from the months. If the delimiter you need is not a single regular expression, you might be able to use the extract() function instead of separate(). With extract() you can use regular expression groups to identify the fields to extract.

```
regexp = "([:digit:]+)" \
         "(?:[:alpha:]|[:space:])+" \
         "[:space:]([:alpha:]+)"
extract(
    tbl, date,
    into = c("day", "month"),
    regex = regexp
)

## # A tibble: 3 x 2
##    day    month
##    <chr>  <chr>
## 1  11     May
## 2  4      July
## 3  21     December
```

The reverse of separating is uniting. For example, let tbl2 contain a day and a month column.

```
tbl <- tribble(
    ~date,
    "11/5",
    "4/7",
    "21/12"
)
tbl2 <- separate(tbl, date, into = c("day", "month"))
```

To create a date column from the day and the month, we use unite(). The col argument should be the column we create and the following columns those we create it from.

```
unite(tbl2, col = "date", day, month)
## # A tibble: 3 x 1
##   date
##   <chr>
## 1 11_5
## 2 4_7
## 3 21_12
```

By default, the separator in the new column will be _. This is not what we want for dates, but we can use the sep argument to change it.

```
unite(tbl2, col = "date", day, month, sep = "/")
## # A tibble: 3 x 1
##   date
##   <chr>
## 1 11/5
## 2 4/7
## 3 21/12
```

If we want to keep the original columns around, we can set the remove argument to FALSE.

```
unite(
    tbl2,
    col = "date", day, month,
    sep = "/", remove = FALSE
)

## # A tibble: 3 x 3
##   date  day   month
##   <chr> <chr> <chr>
## 1 11/5  11    5
## 2 4/7   4     7
## 3 21/12 21    12
```

Columns that contain more than one value do not always contain the same number of values. For example, we could have data such as the number of casualties per major group in WW1 and WW2.

```
military_casualties <- tribble(
    ~war, ~groups, ~deaths,

    'WW1',
    "Allied Powers/Central Powers",
    "5.7,4.0",

    'WW2',
    "Germany/Japan/USSR/British Empire/USA",
    "5.3,2.1,10.7,0.6,0.4"
)
```

The groupings were not the same in the two wars, so we cannot split the data into different columns. We can, however, divide it into more rows using separate_rows().

```
separate_rows(
    military_casualties,
    groups, deaths,
    sep = "/|,"
)

## # A tibble: 7 x 3
##    war    groups          deaths
##    <chr>  <chr>           <chr>
## 1  WW1    Allied Powers   5.7
## 2  WW1    Central Powers  4.0
## 3  WW2    Germany         5.3
## 4  WW2    Japan           2.1
## 5  WW2    USSR            10.7
## 6  WW2    British Empire  0.6
## 7  WW2    USA             0.4
```

Expanding, Crossing, and Completing

For some applications, it is useful to create all combinations of values from two or more columns—even those combinations that are missing from the data. For this, you can use the function expand():

```
tbl <- tribble(
    ~A, ~B, ~C,
     1, 11, 21,
     2, 11, 22,
     4, 13, 32
)
```

```
expand(tbl, A, B)
```

```
## # A tibble: 6 x 2
##        A     B
##    <dbl> <dbl>
## 1      1    11
## 2      1    13
## 3      2    11
## 4      2    13
## 5      4    11
## 6      4    13
```

Here, we get all combinations of values from columns A and B, while column C is ignored. If a column contains values from a larger set than what is found in the data, you can give expand() a vector of values:

```
expand(tbl, A = 1:4, B)
```

```
## # A tibble: 8 x 2
##        A     B
##    <int> <dbl>
## 1      1    11
## 2      1    13
## 3      2    11
## 4      2    13
## 5      3    11
## 6      3    13
## 7      4    11
## 8      4    13
```

If you have vectors of values you want to combine this way, you can also use the crossing() function.

crossing(A = 1:3, B = 11:13)

```
## # A tibble: 9 x 2
##       A     B
##    <int> <int>
## 1     1    11
## 2     1    12
## 3     1    13
## 4     2    11
## 5     2    12
## 6     2    13
## 7     3    11
## 8     3    12
## 9     3    13
```

If you only want the combinations found in the data, you can combine expand() with the nesting() function:

```
tbl <- tribble(
    ~A, ~B, ~C,
    1, 11, 21,
    2, 11, 22,
    2, 11, 12,
    4, 13, 42,
    4, 13, 32
)
expand(tbl, nesting(A, B))
```

```
## # A tibble: 3 x 2
##       A     B
##    <dbl> <dbl>
```

```
## 1       1      11
## 2       2      11
## 3       4      13
```

This combination gives you all the combinations of the specified columns—all other columns are ignored—and only the unique combinations, unlike if you extracted the columns by indexing.

If you need all combinations in a data frame, but accept missing values for those that are not present, you can use the complete() function. It makes sure you have all combinations and put missing values in the remaining columns for the combinations that are not in the original data.

complete(tbl, A = 1:4)

```
## # A tibble: 6 x 3
##        A     B     C
##    <dbl> <dbl> <dbl>
## 1      1    11    21
## 2      2    11    22
## 3      2    11    12
## 4      3    NA    NA
## 5      4    13    42
## 6      4    13    32
```

complete(tbl, B = 11:13)

```
## # A tibble: 6 x 3
##        B     A     C
##    <dbl> <dbl> <dbl>
## 1     11     1    21
## 2     11     2    22
## 3     11     2    12
## 4     12    NA    NA
```

```
## 5     13      4     42
## 6     13      4     32
```

complete(tbl, A = 1:4, B = 11:13)

```
## # A tibble: 14 x 3
##        A      B      C
##     <dbl>  <dbl>  <dbl>
## 1     1     11     21
## 2     1     12     NA
## 3     1     13     NA
## 4     2     11     22
## 5     2     11     12
## 6     2     12     NA
## 7     2     13     NA
## 8     3     11     NA
## 9     3     12     NA
## 10    3     13     NA
## 11    4     11     NA
## 12    4     12     NA
## 13    4     13     42
## 14    4     13     32
```

Missing Values

When data has missing values, it often requires application domain knowledge to deal with it correctly. The tidyr package has some rudimentary support for cleaning data with missing values; you might need more features to deal with missing values properly, and you are likely to find those in the dplyr package; see Chapter 7.

The simplest way to handle missing values is to get rid of it. A crude approach is to remove all observations with one or more missing variable values. The drop_na() function does exactly that.

```
mean_income <- tribble(
    ~country,    ~`2002`,   ~`2003`,   ~`2004`,   ~`2005`,
    "Numenor",   123456,    132654,        NA,    324156,
    "Westeros",  314256,    NA,            NA,    465321,
    "Narnia",    432156,    NA,            NA,        NA,
    "Gondor",    531426,    321465,    235461,    463521,
    "Laputa",     14235,     34125,     45123,     51234,
)
drop_na(mean_income)

## # A tibble: 2 x 5
##    country `2002` `2003` `2004` `2005`
##    <chr>    <dbl>  <dbl>  <dbl>  <dbl>
## 1 Gondor   531426 321465 235461 463521
## 2 Laputa    14235  34125  45123  51234
```

In this example, we lose a country entirely if we have missing data for a single year. This is unlikely to be acceptable and is another good argument for tidy data. If we reformat the table and drop missing values, we will only remove the observations where the income is missing for a given year.

```
tidy_mean_income <- gather(
    data = mean_income,
    key = "year",
    value = "mean_income",
    -country
)
```

```
drop_na(tidy_mean_income)
```

```
## # A tibble: 14 x 3
##     country  year  mean_income
##     <chr>    <chr>       <dbl>
##  1 Numenor  2002       123456
##  2 Westeros 2002       314256
##  3 Narnia   2002       432156
##  4 Gondor   2002       531426
##  5 Laputa   2002        14235
##  6 Numenor  2003       132654
##  7 Gondor   2003       321465
##  8 Laputa   2003        34125
##  9 Gondor   2004       235461
## 10 Laputa   2004        45123
## 11 Numenor  2005       324156
## 12 Westeros 2005       465321
## 13 Gondor   2005       463521
## 14 Laputa   2005        51234
```

Sometimes, you can replace missing data with some appropriate data. For example, we could replace missing data in the mean_income table by setting each value to the mean of its column. The replace_na() function does this. It takes a data frame as its first argument and a list specifying replacements as its second argument. This list should have a name for each column you want to replace missing values in, and the value assigned to these names should be the values with which you wish you replace.

```
replace_na(mean_income, list(
    `2003` = mean(mean_income$`2003`, na.rm = TRUE)
))
```

```
## # A tibble: 5 x 5
##    country  `2002` `2003` `2004` `2005`
##    <chr>     <dbl>  <dbl>  <dbl>  <dbl>
## 1 Numenor   123456 132654     NA 324156
## 2 Westeros  314256 162748     NA 465321
## 3 Narnia    432156 162748     NA     NA
## 4 Gondor    531426 321465 235461 463521
## 5 Laputa     14235  34125  45123  51234
```

```
replace_na(mean_income, list(
    `2003` = mean(mean_income$`2003`, na.rm = TRUE),
    `2004` = mean(mean_income$`2004`, na.rm = TRUE),
    `2005` = mean(mean_income$`2005`, na.rm = TRUE)
))
```

```
## # A tibble: 5 x 5
##    country  `2002` `2003` `2004` `2005`
##    <chr>     <dbl>  <dbl>  <dbl>  <dbl>
## 1 Numenor   123456 132654 140292 324156
## 2 Westeros  314256 162748 140292 465321
## 3 Narnia    432156 162748 140292 326058
## 4 Gondor    531426 321465 235461 463521
## 5 Laputa     14235  34125  45123  51234
```

In this example, using the mean per year is unlikely to be useful; it would make more sense to replace missing data with the mean for each country. This is not immediately possible with tidyr functions, though. With dplyr we have the tools for it and I return to it in Chapter 7.

A final function for managing missing data is the fill() function. It replaces missing values with the value above them in their column (or below them if you set the argument .direction to "up". Imagine that we have a table of income per quarter of each year, but the year is only mentioned for the first quarter.

```
tbl <- read_csv(
    "year, quarter, income
    2011, Q1, 13
    , Q2, 12
    , Q3, 14
    , Q4, 11
    2012, Q1, 12
    , Q2, 14
    , Q3, 15
    , Q4, 17"
)
```

We can repeat the years downward through the quarters with `fill()`:

```
fill(tbl, year)
```

```
## # A tibble: 8 x 3
##     year quarter income
##    <dbl> <chr>    <dbl>
## 1   2011 Q1          13
## 2   2011 Q2          12
## 3   2011 Q3          14
## 4   2011 Q4          11
## 5   2012 Q1          12
## 6   2012 Q2          14
## 7   2012 Q3          15
## 8   2012 Q4          17
```

Nesting Data

A final functionality that `tidyr` provides is nesting data. A tibble entry usually contains simple data, such as numbers or strings, but it can also hold complex data, such as other tables.

Consider this table:

```
tbl <- tribble(
    ~A, ~B, ~C,
    1, 11, 21,
    1, 11, 12,
    2, 42, 22,
    2, 15, 22,
    2, 15, 32,
    4, 13, 32
)
```

From this table, we can create one that, for each value in the A column, contains a table of B and C for that A value.

```
nested_tbl <- nest(tbl, B, C)
nested_tbl

## # A tibble: 3 x 2
##       A data
##   <dbl> <list>
## 1     1 <tibble [2 x 2]>
## 2     2 <tibble [3 x 2]>
## 3     4 <tibble [1 x 2]>

nested_tbl[[1,2]]

## # A tibble: 2 x 2
##       B     C
##   <dbl> <dbl>
```

```
## 1     11     21
## 2     11     12
```

The column that contains the nested table is named data, but you can change this using the .key argument.

```
nested_tbl <- nest(tbl, B, C, .key = "BC")
nested_tbl
```

```
## # A tibble: 3 x 2
##       A  BC
##    <dbl> <list>
## 1      1 <tibble [2 × 2]>
## 2      2 <tibble [3 × 2]>
## 3      4 <tibble [1 × 2]>
```

```
nested_tbl$BC
```

```
## [[1]]
## # A tibble: 2 x 2
##       B     C
##    <dbl> <dbl>
## 1     11    21
## 2     11    12
##
## [[2]]
## # A tibble: 3 x 2
##       B     C
##    <dbl> <dbl>
## 1     42    22
## 2     15    22
## 3     15    32
##
## [[3]]
```

```
## # A tibble: 1 x 2
##        B     C
##    <dbl> <dbl>
## 1     13    32
```

The arguments after the table pick the columns to be nested. You can use any number of columns here, including no columns at all. In the latter case, you will nest the entire original table in the data column.

nest(tbl, B)

```
## # A tibble: 5 x 3
##        A     C data
##    <dbl> <dbl> <list>
## 1     1    21 <tibble [1 x 1]>
## 2     1    12 <tibble [1 x 1]>
## 3     2    22 <tibble [2 x 1]>
## 4     2    32 <tibble [1 x 1]>
## 5     4    32 <tibble [1 x 1]>
```

nest(tbl)

```
## # A tibble: 1 x 1
##    data
##    <list>
## 1 <tibble [6 x 3]>
```

The reverse operation is unnest():

nested_tbl

```
## # A tibble: 3 x 2
##        A BC
##    <dbl> <list>
## 1     1 <tibble [2 x 2]>
```

```
## 2      2 <tibble [3 × 2]>
## 3      4 <tibble [1 × 2]>
```

unnest(nested_tbl)

```
## # A tibble: 6 × 3
##        A     B     C
##    <dbl> <dbl> <dbl>
## 1     1    11    21
## 2     1    11    12
## 3     2    42    22
## 4     2    15    22
## 5     2    15    32
## 6     4    13    32
```

Nesting is not a typical operation in data analysis, but it is there if you need it, and in the packages in Chapter 11 we see some usages.

CHAPTER 5

Pipelines: `magrittr`

Data analysis consists of several steps, where your data moves through different stages of transformations and cleaning before you finally get to model construction. In practical terms, this means that your R code will consist of a series of function calls where the output of one is the input of the next. The pattern is typical, but a straightforward implementation of it has several drawbacks. The Tidyverse provides a "pipe operator" to alleviate this.

The pipe operator is implemented in the `magrittr` package. You can load it as part of the `tidyverse` package:

```
library(tidyverse)
```

Or you can explicitly load the package:

```
library(magrittr)
```

If you load `magrittr` through the `tidyverse` package, you will get the most common pipe operator, %>%, but not alternative ones—see the following. For those, you need to load `magrittr`.

The Problem with Pipelines

Consider this data from Chapter 4.

```
write_csv(
    tribble(
        ~country,  ~`2002`, ~`2003`, ~`2004`, ~`2005`,
        "Numenor", 123456, 132654,      NA, 324156,
```

```
        "Westeros", 314256,  NA,            NA,  465321,
        "Narnia",   432156,  NA,            NA,      NA,
        "Gondor",   531426,  321465,  235461,  463521,
        "Laputa",    14235,   34125,   45123,   51234,
  ),
  "data/income.csv"
)
```

I have written it to a file, data/income.csv, to make the following examples easier to read.

In Chapter 4 we reformatted and cleaned this data using gather() and drop_na():

```
mydata <- read_csv("data/income.csv",
                   col_types = "cdddd")
mydata <- gather(
    data = mydata,
    key = "year",
    value = "mean_income",
    -country
)
mydata <- drop_na(mydata)
```

This is a typical pipeline, although a short one. It consists of three steps: 1) read the data into R, 2) tidy the data, and 3) clean the data.

There is nothing inherently wrong with code like this. Each step is easy to read; it is a function call that transforms your data from one form to another. The pipelined nature of the code, however, is not explicit. We can read the code and see that the output of one function is the input of the next, but what if it isn't?

Consider this:

```
mydata <- read_csv("data/income.csv",
                    col_types = "cdddd")
data <- gather(...) # Are we assigning to the right name?
mydata <- drop_na(mydata) # Input from read_csv() not gather()
```

The result of gather() is assigned to the variable data and then drop_na() is called on mydata. If our intent were the preceding pipeline, this would be a mistake. But maybe we wanted the result of gather() to be a separate data table needed for some downstream analysis.

A series of transformation steps that constitute a pipeline can only be recognized as such by following programming conventions, and unless the code is well documented and well understood, we cannot immediately see from the code whether assigning to data instead of mydata is an error.

We can make pipelines more explicit. If the output of one function should be the input of the next, we can nest the function calls:

```
mydata <- drop_na(
    gather(
        data = read_csv("data/income.csv",
                        col_types = "cdddd"),
        key = "year",
        value = "mean_income",
        -country
    )
)
```

This makes the pipeline intention explicit but the code very hard to read; you have to work out the pipeline from the innermost function call to the outermost.

The magrittr package gives us notation for explicitly describing specifying readable pipelines.

Pipeline Notation

The pipeline operator, %>%, introduces syntactic sugar for function calls.[1]
The code

x %>% **f**()

is equivalent to

f(x)

and

x %>% **f**() %>% **g**() %>% **h**()

is equivalent to

h(**g**(**f**(x)))

So, by the way, is

x %>% f %>% g %>% h

You do not need the parentheses for the function calls, but most prefer
them to make it clear that we are dealing with functions. Also, if your
functions take more than one argument, parentheses are needed, so if you
always include them, it gives you a consistent notation.

---

[1]The pipeline operator is syntactic sugar in the sense that it introduces a more
readable notation for a function call. In compiled languages, syntactic sugar
would be directly translated into the original form and have exactly the same
runtime behavior as the sugar-free version. In R, there is no compile-time phase,
so you pay a runtime cost for all syntactic sugar. The pipe operator is a complex
function, so compared to explicit function calls, it is slow to use it. This is rarely an
issue, though, since the expensive data processing is done inside the function and
not in function calls.

The preceding nested function call pipeline

```
mydata <- drop_na(gather(read_csv(...)))
```

can thus be rewritten in pipe form

```
mydata <- read_csv(...) %>% gather(...) %>% drop_na()
```

or, with all the arguments included, as

```
mydata <- read_csv("data/income.csv",
                   col_types = "cdddd") %>%
   gather(key = "year", value = "mean_income", -country) %>%
   drop_na()
```

The pipeline notation combines the readability of single function call steps with explicit notation for data processing pipelines.

Pipelines and Function Arguments

The pipe operator is left-associative, that is, it evaluates from left to right, and the expression lhs %>% rhs expects the left-hand side (lhs) to be data and the right-hand side (rhs) to be a function. The result will be rhs(lhs). The output of this function call is the left-hand side of the next pipe operator in the pipeline or the result of the entire pipeline. If the right-hand side function takes more than one argument, you provide these in the rhs expression. The expression

```
lhs %>% rhs(x, y, z)
```

will be evaluated as the function call

```
rhs(lhs, x, y, z)
```

By default, the left-hand side is given as the first argument to the right-hand side function. The arguments that you explicitly write on the right-hand side expression are the additional function parameters.

You can change the default using the special variable . (dot). If the right-hand side expression has . as a parameter, then that is where the left-hand side value goes. All the following three pipelines are equivalent:

```
mydata <- read_csv("data/income.csv", col_types = "cdddd") %>%
    gather(key = "year", value = "mean_income", -country) %>%
    drop_na()

mydata <- read_csv("data/income.csv", col_types = "cdddd") %>%
    gather(data = ., key = "year", value = "mean_income", -country) %>%
    drop_na()

mydata <- read_csv("data/income.csv", col_types = "cdddd") %>%
    gather(key = "year", value = "mean_income", -country, data
    = .) %>%
    drop_na()
```

You can use dot more than once on the right-hand side:

```
rnorm(5) %>% tibble(x = ., y = .)

## # A tibble: 5 x 2
##          x        y
##      <dbl>    <dbl>
## 1 -0.620   -0.620
## 2  0.0349   0.0349
## 3 -0.183   -0.183
## 4  2.17     2.17
## 5 -1.37    -1.37
```

You can also use it in nested function calls.

```
rnorm(5) %>% tibble(x = ., y = abs(.))
```

```
## # A tibble: 5 x 2
##        x     y
##    <dbl> <dbl>
## 1 -0.881 0.881
## 2  1.42  1.42
## 3  0.493 0.493
## 4  1.04  1.04
## 5 -1.56  1.56
```

If the dot is *only* found in nested function calls, however, magrittr will still add it as the first argument to the right-hand side function.

```
rnorm(5) %>% tibble(x = sin(.), y = abs(.))
```

```
## # A tibble: 5 x 3
##        .      x     y
##    <dbl>  <dbl> <dbl>
## 1 -0.372 -0.363 0.372
## 2 -0.730 -0.667 0.730
## 3  0.202  0.201 0.202
## 4  0.642  0.599 0.642
## 5  0.516  0.493 0.516
```

To avoid this, you can put the right-hand side expression in curly brackets:

```
rnorm(5) %>% { tibble(x = sin(.), y = abs(.)) }
```

```
## # A tibble: 5 x 2
##           x       y
##       <dbl>   <dbl>
## 1   0.364   0.372
## 2  -0.855   1.03
## 3  -0.141   0.141
## 4   0.172   0.173
## 5  -0.0462  0.0462
```

In general, you can put expressions in curly brackets as the right-hand side of a pipe operator and have magrittr evaluate them. Think of it as a way to write one-parameter anonymous functions. The input variable is the dot, and the expression inside the curly brackets is the body of the function.

Function Composition

It is trivial to write your own functions such that they work well with pipelines. All functions map input to output (ideally with no side effects) so all functions can be used in a pipeline. If the key input is the first argument of a function you write, the default placement of left-hand side value will work—so that is preferable—but otherwise you can explicitly use the dot.

When writing pipelines, however, often you do not need to write a function from scratch. If a function is merely a composition of other function calls—it is a pipeline function itself—we can define it as such.

In mathematics, the function composition operator, $\circ$, defines the composition of functions f and g, $g \circ f$ to be the function

$$(g \circ f)(x) = g(f(x))$$

Many functional programming languages encourage you to write functions by combining other functions and have operators for that. It is not frequently done in R, and while you can implement function composition, there is no built-in operator. The `magrittr` package, however, gives you this syntax:

```
h <- . %>% f() %>% g()
```

This defines the function h, such that `h(x)` = `g(f(x))`.

If we take the tidy-then-clean pipeline we saw previously, and imagine that we need to do the same for several input files, we can define a pipeline function for this as

```
pipeline <- . %>%
    gather(key = "year", value = "mean_income", -country) %>%
    drop_na()
```

Other Pipe Operations

There are three other pipe operators in `magrittr`. These are not imported when you import the `tidyverse` package, so to get access to them, you have to import `magrittr` explicitly.

```
library(magrittr)
```

The `%<>%` operator is used to run a pipeline starting with a variable and ending by assigning the result of the pipeline back to that variable.

The code

```
mydata <- read_csv("data/income.csv",
                   col_types = "cdddd")
mydata %<>% pipeline()
```

is equivalent to

```
mydata <- read_csv("data/income.csv",
                   col_types = "cdddd")
mydata <- mydata %>% pipeline()
```

This reassignment operator behaves similarly to the step-wise pipeline convention we considered at the start of the chapter, but it makes explicit that we are updating an existing variable. You cannot accidentally assign the result to a different variable.

If your right-hand side is an expression in curly brackets, you can refer to the input through the dot variable:

```
mydata <- tibble(x = rnorm(5), y = rnorm(5))
mydata %>% { .$x - .$y }
```

```
## [1]  0.9590534  1.9584677 -0.9095741 -1.8365738
## [5] -0.7331230
```

If, as here, the input is a data frame and you want to access its columns, you need the notation .$ to access them. The %$% pipe operator opens the data frame for you so you can refer to the columns by name.

```
mydata %$% { x - y }
```

```
## [1]  0.9590534  1.9584677 -0.9095741 -1.8365738
## [5] -0.7331230
```

The *tee*-pipe operator, %T>%, behaves like the regular pipe operator, %>%, except that it returns its input rather than the result of calling the function on its right-hand side. The regular pipe operation x %>% f() will return f(x), but the tee-pipe operation, x %T>% f(), will call f(x) but return x. This is useful for calling functions with side effects as a step inside a pipeline, such as saving intermediate results to files or plotting data.

If you call a function in a usual pipeline, you will pass the result of the function call on to the next function in the pipeline. If you, for example, want to plot intermediate data, you might not be so lucky that the plotting function will return the data. The ggplot2 functions will not (see Chapter 12).

If you want to plot intermediate values, you need to save the data in a variable, save it, and then start a new pipeline with the data as input.

```
income <- read_csv("data/income.csv", col_types = "cdddd")
tidy_income <- gather(income, key = "year",
                      value = "mean_income", -country)
ggplot(tidy_income, aes(x = year, y = mean_income))
write_csv(tidy_income, "data/tidy-income.csv")
```

With the tee operator, you can call the plotting function and continue the pipeline.

```
mydata <- mean_income %>%
    gather(key = "year", value = "mean_income", -country) %T>%
    { print(ggplot(., aes(x = year, y = mean_income)) +
            geom_point()) } %>%
    drop_na()
```

CHAPTER 6

Functional Programming: `purrr`

A pipeline-based approach to data processing necessitates a functional programming approach. After all, pipelines are compositions of functions, and loops and variable assignment do not work well with pipelines. You are not precluded from imperative programming, but you need to wrap it in functions.

The package `purrr` makes functional programming easier. As with the other packages in this book, it will be loaded if you import `tidyverse`, but you can load it explicitly with:

```
library(purrr)
```

I will not describe all the functions in the `purrr` package; there are many and more could be added between the time I write this and the time you read it, but I will describe the functions you will likely use often.

Many of the examples in this chapter are so trivial that you would not use `purrr` for them. Many reduce to vector expressions, and vector expressions are both more straightforward to read and faster to evaluate. However, applications where you cannot use vector expressions are more involved, and I do not want the examples to overshadow the syntax.

© Thomas Mailund 2019
T. Mailund, *R Data Science Quick Reference*, https://doi.org/10.1007/978-1-4842-4894-2_6

General Features of `purrr` Functions

The functions in the `purrr` package are "high-order" functions, which means that the functions either take other functions as input or return functions when you call them (or both). Most of the functions take data as their first argument and return modified data. Thus, they are immediately useable with `magrittr` pipelines. As additional arguments, they will accept one or more functions that specify how you want to translate the input into the output.

Other functions do not transform data but instead modify functions. These are used, so you do not need to write functions for the data transformation functions explicitly; you can use a small set of functions and adapt them where needed.

Filtering

One of the most straightforward functional programming patterns is filtering. Here, you use a high-order filter function. This function takes a predicate function, that is, a function that returns a logical value, and then returns all elements where the predicate evaluates to TRUE (the function `keep()`) or all elements where the predicate evaluates to FALSE (the function `discard()`).

```
is_even <- function(x) x %% 2 == 0
1:6 %>% keep(is_even)

## [1] 2 4 6

1:6 %>% discard(is_even)

## [1] 1 3 5
```

When you work with predicates, the negate() function can come in handy. It changes the truth-value of your predicate, such that if your predicate, p, returns TRUE, then negate(p) returns FALSE and vice versa.

```
1:6 %>% keep(negate(is_even))
```

```
## [1] 1 3 5
```

```
1:6 %>% discard(negate(is_even))
```

```
## [1] 2 4 6
```

Since you already have complementary functions in keep() and discard(), you would not use negate() for filtering, though.

A special-case function, compact(), removes NULL elements from a list.

```
y <- list(NULL, 1:3, NULL)
y %>% compact()
```

```
## [[1]]
## [1] 1 2 3
```

If you access attributes on objects, and those are not set, R will give you NULL as a result, and for such cases, compact() can be useful.

If we define lists

```
x <- y <- 1:3
names(y) <- c("one", "two", "three")
```

then y's values will be named, while x's will not. If we try to get the names from x, we will get NULL.

```
names(x)
```

```
## NULL
```

```
names(y)
```

```
## [1] "one" "two" "three"
```

Using compact() with names(), we will discard x.

```
z <- list(x, y)
z %>% compact()
```

```
## [[1]]
## [1] 1 2 3
##
## [[2]]
## one two three
##   1   2     3
```

```
z %>% compact(names)
```

```
## [[1]]
## one two three
##   1   2     3
```

Mapping

Mapping a function, *f*, over a sequence $x = x_1, x_2, \ldots, x_n$ returns a new sequence of the same length as the input but where each element is an application of the function: $f(x_1), f(x_2), \ldots, f(x_n)$.

The function map() does this and return a list as output. Lists are the generic sequence data structure in R since they can hold all types of R objects.

```
is_even <- function(x) x %% 2 == 0
1:4 %>% map(is_even)
```

```
## [[1]]
## [1] FALSE
##
## [[2]]
## [1] TRUE
##
```

```
## [[3]]
## [1] FALSE
##
## [[4]]
## [1] TRUE
```

Often we want to work with vectors of specific types. For all the atomic types, purrr has a specific mapping function. The function for logical values is named map_lgl().

```
is_even <- function(x) x %% 2 == 0
1:4 %>% map_lgl(is_even)
```

```
## [1] FALSE TRUE FALSE TRUE
```

With something as simple as this example, you should not use purrr. Vector expressions are faster and easier to use.

```
1:4 %% 2 == 0
```

```
## [1] FALSE TRUE FALSE TRUE
```

You cannot always use vector expressions, however. Say you want to sample *n* elements from a normal distribution, for a sequence of different *n* values, and then calculate the standard error of the mean. The vector expression

```
sd(rnorm(n = n)) / sqrt(n) # not SEM!
```

does not compute this. If you give rnorm() a sequence for its n parameter, it takes the *length* of the input as the number of elements to sample.

```
n <- seq.int(100, 1000, 300)
rnorm(n) # length(n) is used for n!
```

```
## [1]  1.0642869  0.6745540 -0.1342023 -0.3390898
```

When you have a function that is not vectorized, you can use a map function to apply it on all elements in a list.

```
sem <- function(n) sd(rnorm(n = n)) / sqrt(n)
n %>% map_dbl(sem)
```

```
## [1] 0.10643498 0.04872984 0.03715846 0.03247213
```

Here, I used map_dbl() to get doubles (numerics) as output. The functions map_chr() and map_int() will give you strings and integers instead.

```
1:3 %>% map_dbl(identity) %T>% print() %>% class()
```

```
## [1] 1 2 3
```

```
## [1] "numeric"
```

```
1:3 %>% map_chr(identity) %T>% print() %>% class()
```

```
## [1] "1" "2" "3"
```

```
## [1] "character"
```

```
1:3 %>% map_int(identity) %T>% print() %>% class()
```

```
## [1] 1 2 3
```

```
## [1] "integer"
```

The different map functions will give you an error if the function you apply does not return values of the type the function should. Sometimes a map function will do type conversion, as presented earlier, but not always. It will usually be happy to convert in a direction that doesn't lose information, for example, from logical to integer and integer to double, but not in the other direction.

For example, map_lgl() will not convert from integers to logical if you give it the identity() function, even though you can convert these types. Similarly, you can convert strings to integers using as.numeric(), but map_dbl() will not do so if we give it identity(). The mapping functions are more strict than the base R conversion functions. So you should use functions that give you the right type.

The map_dfr() and map_dfc() functions return data frames (tibbles). The function you map should return data frames and these will be combined, row-wise with map_dfr() and column-wise with map_dfc().

```
x <- tibble(a = 1:2, b = 3:4)
list(a = x, b = x) %>% map_dfr(identity)

## # A tibble: 4 x 2
##        a     b
##    <int> <int>
## 1     1     3
## 2     2     4
## 3     1     3
## 4     2     4

list(a = x, b = x) %>% map_dfc(identity)

## # A tibble: 2 x 4
##        a     b    a1    b1
##    <int> <int> <int> <int>
## 1     1     3     1     3
## 2     2     4     2     4
```

The map_df() function does the same as map_dfr():

```
list(a = x, b = x) %>% map_df(identity)
## # A tibble: 4 x 2
##       a     b
##    <int> <int>
## 1     1     3
## 2     2     4
## 3     1     3
## 4     2     4
```

You do not need to give the data frame functions data frames as input, as long as the function you apply to the input returns data frames. This goes for all the map functions. They will accept any sequence input; they only restrict and convert the output.

If the items you map over are sequences themselves, you can extract elements by index; you do not need to provide a function to the map function.

```
x <- list(1:3, 4:6)
x %>% map_dbl(1)

## [1] 1 4

x %>% map_dbl(3)

## [1] 3 6
```

If the items have names, you can also extract values using these.

```
x <- list(
    c(a = 42, b = 13),
    c(a = 24, b = 31)
)
```

```
x %>% map_dbl("a")
```

```
## [1] 42 24
```

```
x %>% map_dbl("b")
```

```
## [1] 13 31
```

This is mostly used when you map over data frames.

```
a <- tibble(foo = 1:3, bar = 11:13)
b <- tibble(foo = 4:6, bar = 14:16)
ab <- list(a, b)
ab %>% map("foo")
```

```
## [[1]]
## [1] 1 2 3
##
## [[2]]
## [1] 4 5 6
```

Related to extracting elements by name or index, you can apply functions to different depths of the input using map_depth(). Depth zero is the list itself, so mapping over this depth is the same as applying the function directly on the input.

```
ab %>% map_depth(0, length)
```

```
## [1] 2
```

```
ab %>% length()
```

```
## [1] 2
```

Depth 1 gives us each element in the sequence, so this behaves like a normal map. Depth 2 provides us with a map over the nested elements. Consider the preceding list ab. The top level, depth 0, is the list. Depth 1

is the data frames a and b. Depth 2 is the columns in these data frames.
Depth 3 is the individual items in these columns.

```
ab %>% map_depth(1, sum) %>% unlist()
```

```
## [1] 42 60
```

```
ab %>% map_depth(2, sum) %>% unlist()
```

```
## foo bar foo bar
##   6  36  15  45
```

```
ab %>% map_depth(3, sum) %>% unlist()
```

```
## foo1 foo2 foo3 bar1 bar2 bar3 foo1 foo2 foo3 bar1
##    1    2    3   11   12   13    4    5    6   14
## bar2 bar3
##   15   16
```

If you only want to apply a function to some of the elements, you can
use map_if(). It takes a predicate and a function and applies the function
to those elements where the predicate is true. It returns a list, but you can
convert it if you want another type.

```
is_even <- function(x) x %% 2 == 0
add_one <- function(x) x + 1
1:6 %>% map_if(is_even, add_one) %>% as.numeric()
```

```
## [1] 1 3 3 5 5 7
```

Notice that this is different from combining filtering and mapping; that
combination would remove the elements that do not satisfy the predicate.

```
1:6 %>% keep(is_even) %>% map_dbl(add_one)
```

```
## [1] 3 5 7
```

With map_if(), you keep all elements, but the function is only applied to some of them.

If you want to apply one function to the elements where the predicate is true and another to the elements where it is false, you can prove a function to the .else element:

```
add_two <- function(x) x + 2
1:6 %>%
    map_if(is_even, add_one, .else = add_two) %>%
    as.numeric()
```

```
## [1] 3 3 5 5 7 7
```

If you know which indices you want to apply the function to, instead of a predicate they must satisfy, you can use map_at(). This function takes a sequence of indices instead of the predicate but otherwise works the same as map_if().

```
1:6 %>% map_at(2:5, add_one) %>% as.numeric()
```

```
## [1] 1 3 4 5 6 6
```

If you map over a list, x, then your function will be called with the elements in the list, x[[i]]. If you want to get the elements wrapped in a length-one list, that is, use indexing x[i], you can use lmap().

```
list(1:3, 4:6) %>% map(print) %>% invisible()
```

```
## [1] 1 2 3
## [1] 4 5 6
```

```
list(1:3, 4:6) %>% lmap(print) %>% invisible()
```

```
## [[1]]
## [1] 1 2 3
##
## [[1]]
## [1] 4 5 6
```

The function you apply must always return a list, and lmap() will concatenate them.

```
f <- function(x) list("foo")
1:2 %>% lmap(f)
```

```
## [[1]]
## [1] "foo"
##
## [[2]]
## [1] "foo"
```

```
f <- function(x) list("foo", "bar")
1:2 %>% lmap(f)
```

```
## [[1]]
## [1] "foo"
##
## [[2]]
## [1] "bar"
##
## [[3]]
## [1] "foo"
##
## [[4]]
## [1] "bar"
```

For example, while you can get the length of elements in a list using map() and length()

```
list(1:3, 4:6) %>% map(length) %>% unlist()
```

```
## [1] 3 3
```

you will get an error if you try the same using lmap(). This is because length() returns a numeric and not a list. You need to wrap length() with list() so the result is the length in a (length-one) list.

```
wrapped_length <- . %>% length %>% list()
list(1:3, 4:6) %>% lmap(wrapped_length) %>% unlist()
```

```
## [1] 1 1
```

If it surprises you that the lengths are one here, remember that the function is called with the length-one lists at each index. If you want the length of what they contain, you need to extract that.

```
wrapped_length <- . %>% .[[1]] %>% length %>% list()
list(1:3, 4:6) %>% lmap(wrapped_length) %>% unlist()
```

```
## [1] 3 3
```

If you want to extract the nested data, though, you probably want map() and not lmap().

The functions lmap_if() and lmap_at() work as map_if() and map_at() except for how they index the input and handle the output as lists to be concatenated.

Sometimes, we only want to call a function for its side effect. In that case, you can pipe the result of a map into invisible(). The function walk() does that for you, and using it makes it explicit that this is what you want, but it is simply syntactic sugar for map() + invisible()

```
1:3 %>% map(print) %>% invisible()
```

```
## [1] 1
## [1] 2
## [1] 3
```

```
1:3 %>% walk(print)
```

```
## [1] 1
## [1] 2
## [1] 3
```

If you need to map over multiple sequences, you have two choices of map functions to choose from. Some functions map over exactly two sequences. For each of the map() functions, there are similar map2() functions. These take two sequences as the first two arguments.

```
x <- 1:3
y <- 3:1
map2_dbl(x, y, `+`)
```

```
## [1] 4 4 4
```

You can also create lists of sequences and use the pmap() functions.

```
list(x, y) %>% pmap_dbl(`+`)
```

```
## [1] 4 4 4
```

There are the same type-specific versions as there are for map() and map2(), but with the pmap() functions, you can map over more than one or two input sequences.

```
z <- 4:6
f <- function(x, y, z) x + y - z
list(x, y, z) %>% pmap_dbl(f)
```

```
## [1] 0 -1 -2
```

If you need to know the indices for each value you map over, you can use the imap() variations. When you use these to map over a sequence, your function needs to take two arguments where the first argument is the sequence value and the second the value's index in the input.

```
x <- c("foo", "bar", "baz")
f <- function(x, i) paste0(i, ": ", x)
x %>% imap_chr(f)
```

```
## [1] "1: foo" "2: bar" "3: baz"
```

There is yet another variant of the mapping functions, the modify()
functions. These do not have the type variants (but the _at, _if, _depth,
and so on); instead, they will always give you an output of the same type as
the input:

```
modify2(1:3, 3:1, `+`)
```

```
## [1] 4 4 4
```

```
x <- c("foo", "bar", "baz")
f <- function(x, i) paste0(i, ": ", x)
x %>% imodify(f)
```

```
## [1] "1: foo" "2: bar" "3: baz"
```

Reduce and Accumulate

If you want to summarize all your input into a single value, you probably
want to reduce() them. Reduce repeatedly applies a function over your
input sequence: If you have a function of two arguments, $f(a, x)$ and a
sequence $x_1, x_2, \ldots, x_n$, then reduce(f) will compute $f(\ldots f(f(x_1, x_2, x_3), \ldots$
$,x_n), x_n)$, that is, it will be called on the first two elements of the sequence,
the result will be paired with the next element, and so forth. Think of the
argument a as an accumulator that keeps the result of the calculation so far.

To make the order of function application clear, I define a "pair" type:

```
pair <- function(first, second) {
    structure(list(first = first, second = second),
              class = "pair")
}
```

```r
toString.pair <- function(x, ...) {
    first <- toString(x$first, ...)
    rest <- toString(x$second, ...)
    paste('[', first, ', ', rest, ']', sep = ' ')
}
print.pair <- function(x, ...) {
    x %>% toString() %>% cat() %>% invisible()
}
```

If we reduce using pair(), we see how the values are paired when the function is called:

```r
1:4 %>% reduce(pair)
```

```
## [[[1, 2], 3], 4]
```

If you reverse the input, you can reduce in the opposite order, combining the last pair first and propagating the accumulator in that order.

```r
1:4 %>% rev() %>% reduce(pair)
```

```
## [[[4, 3], 2], 1]
```

If, for some reason, you want to apply the function *and* have the accumulator as the last argument, you can use the .dir = "backward" argument.

```r
1:4 %>% reduce(pair, .dir = "backward")
```

```
## [1, [2, [3, 4]]]
```

The first (or last) element in the input does not have to be the value for the initial accumulator. If you want a specific starting value, you can pass that to reduce() using the .init argument.

```r
1:3 %>% reduce(pair, .init = 0)
```

```
## [[[0, 1], 2], 3]
```

```
1:3 %>% rev() %>% reduce(pair, .init = 4)
```

```
## [[[4, 3], 2], 1]
```

```
1:3 %>% reduce(pair, .init = 4, .dir = "backward")
```

```
## [1, [2, [3, 4]]]
```

If your function takes more than one argument, you can provide the additional arguments to reduce() and then input sequence and function. Consider, for example, a three-argument function like this:

```
# additional arguments
loud_pair <- function(acc, next_val, volume) {
    ret <- pair(acc, next_val)
    ret %>% toString() %>%
        paste(volume, '\n', sep = ' ') %>%
        cat()
    ret
}
```

It builds a pair object but, as a side effect, prints the pair followed by a string that indicates how "loud" the printed value is. We can provide the volume as an extra argument to reduce():

```
1:3 %>%
    reduce(loud_pair, volume = '!') %>%
    invisible()
```

```
## [1, 2]!
## [[1, 2], 3]!
```

```
1:3 %>%
    reduce(loud_pair, volume = '!!') %>%
    invisible()
```

```
## [1, 2]!!
## [[1, 2], 3]!!
```

If you want to reduce two sequences instead of one—similar to a second argument to reduce() but a sequence instead of a single value—you can use reduce2():

```
volumes <- c('!', '!!')
1:3 %>% reduce2(volumes, loud_pair) %>% invisible()
```

```
## [1, 2]!
## [[1, 2], 3]!!
```

```
1:3 %>%
    reduce2(c('!', '!!', '!!!!'), .init = 0, loud_pair) %>%
    invisible()
```

```
## [0, 1]!
## [[0, 1], 2]!!
## [[[0, 1], 2], 3]!!!
```

If you want all the intermediate values of the reductions, you can use the accumulate() function. It returns a sequence of the results of each function application.

```
res <- 1:3 %>% accumulate(pair)
print(res[[1]])
```

```
## [1] 1
```

```
print(res[[2]])
```

```
## [1, 2]
```

```
print(res[[3]])
```

```
## [[1, 2], 3]
```

```
res <- 1:3 %>% accumulate(pair, .init = 0)
print(res[[1]])
```

```
## [1] 0
```

```
print(res[[4]])
```

```
## [[[0, 1], 2], 3]
```

```
res <- 1:3 %>% accumulate(
    pair, .init = 0,
    .dir = "backward"
)
print(res[[1]])
```

```
## [1, [2, [3, 0]]]
```

```
print(res[[4]])
```

```
## [1] 0
```

The accumulate2() function works like reduce2(), except that it keeps the intermediate values like accumulate() does.

Partial Evaluation and Function Composition

When you filter, map, or reduce over sequences, you sometimes want to modify a function to match the interface of purrr's functions. If you have a function that takes too many arguments for the interface, but where you can fix some of the parameters to get the application you want, you can do what is called a *partial evaluation*. This just means that you create a new function that calls the original function with some of the parameters fixed.

For example, if you filter, you want a function that takes one input value and returns one (boolean) output value. If you want to filter the values that are less than or greater than, say three, you can create functions for this.

```
greater_than_three <- function(x) 3 < x
less_than_three <- function(x) x < 3

1:6 %>% keep(greater_than_three)

## [1] 4 5 6

1:6 %>% keep(less_than_three)

## [1] 1 2
```

The drawback of doing this is that you might need to define many such functions, even if you only use each once in your pipeline.

Using the partial() function, you can bind parameters without explicitly defining new functions. For example, to bind the first parameter to <, as in the greater_than_three() function, you can use partial():

```
1:6 %>% keep(partial(`<`, 3))

## [1] 4 5 6
```

By default, you always bind the first parameter(s). To bind others, you need to name which parameters to bind. The less-than operator has these parameter names

```
`<`

## function (e1, e2) .Primitive("<")
```

so you can use this partial evaluation for less_than_three():

```
1:6 %>% keep(partial(`<`, e2 = 3))

## [1] 1 2
```

Similarly, you can use partial evaluation for mapping:

```
1:6 %>% map_dbl(partial(`+`, 2))
```

```
## [1] 3 4 5 6 7 8
```

```
1:6 %>% map_dbl(partial(`-`, 1))
```

```
## [1] 0 -1 -2 -3 -4 -5
```

```
1:3 %>% map_dbl(partial(`-`, e1 = 4))
```

```
## [1] 3 2 1
```

```
1:3 %>% map_dbl(partial(`-`, e2 = 4))
```

```
## [1] -3 -2 -1
```

If you need to apply more than one function, for example

```
1:3 %>%
    map_dbl(partial(`+`, 2)) %>%
    map_dbl(partial(`*`, 3))
```

```
## [1] 9 12 15
```

you can also simply combine the functions. The function composition, $\circ$, works as this: $(g \circ f)(x) = g(f(x))$. So the preceding pipeline can also be written as

```
1:3 %>% map_dbl(
    compose(partial(`*`, 3), partial(`+`, 2))
)
```

```
## [1] 9 12 15
```

With partial() and combine(), you can modify functions, but using them does not exactly give you code that is easy to read. A more readable alternative is using *lambda expressions*.

Lambda Expressions

Lambda expressions are a concise syntax for defining anonymous functions, that is, functions that we do not name. The name "lambda expressions" comes from "lambda calculus,"[1] a discipline in formal logic, but in computer science, it is mostly used as a synonym for anonymous functions. In some programming languages, you cannot create anonymous functions; you need to name a function to define it. In other languages, you have special syntax for lambda expressions. In R, you define anonymous functions the same way that you define named functions. You always define functions the same way; you only give them a name when you assign a function definition to a variable.

If this sounds too theoretical, consider this example. When we filtered values that are even, we defined a function, is_even(), to use as a predicate.

```
is_even <- function(x) x %% 2 == 0
1:6 %>% keep(is_even)
```

```
## [1] 2 4 6
```

We defined the function using the expression function(x) x %% 2 == 0 and then we assigned the function to the name is_even. Instead of assigning the function to a name, we could use the function definition directly in the call to keep():

```
1:6 %>% keep(function(x) x %% 2 == 0)
```

```
## [1] 2 4 6
```

---

[1]The name comes from the syntax for functions that uses the Greek letter lambda, λ. A function that adds two to its argument would be written as $\lambda x.x + 2$.

So, R already has lambda expressions, but the syntax is verbose. In purrr, you can use a formula as a lambda expression. You can define an is_even() function using a formula like this

```
is_even_lambda <- ~ .x %% 2 == 0
1:6 %>% keep(is_even_lambda)
```

```
## [1] 2 4 6
```

or use the formula directly in your pipeline.

```
1:6 %>% keep(~ .x %% 2 == 0)
```

```
## [1] 2 4 6
```

The variable .x in the expression will be interpreted as the first argument to the lambda expression.

Lambda expressions are not an approach you can use to define functions in general. They only work because purrr functions understand formulae as function specifications. You cannot write

```
is_even_lambda <- ~ .x %% 2 == 0
is_even_lambda(3)
```

This will give you an error. The error message is not telling you that you try to use a formula as a function, unfortunately, but just that it cannot find the function is_even_lambda. This is because R will look for a function when you call a variable as a function and ignore other variables with the same name. If you reassign to a variable

```
f <- function(x) 2 * x
f <- 5
f(2)
```

```
## Error in f(2): could not find function "f"
```

105

you are told that it cannot find a function with the name you call—not that the variable does not refer to a non-function. That is the error you get if you attempt to call a lambda expression outside a purrr function.

R's rule for looking for functions can be even more confusing if there is a variable in an inner scope and a function in an outer scope:

```
f <- function(x) 2 * x
g <- function() {
    f <- 5 # not a function
    f(2) # will look for a function
}
g()
```

```
## [1] 4
```

Here, the f() function in the outer scope is called because it is a function; the variable in the inner scope is ignored.

Getting back to lambda expressions in purrr functions, you can use them as more readable versions of partial evaluation.

```
1:4 %>% map_dbl(~ .x / 2)
```

```
## [1] 0.5 1.0 1.5 2.0
```

```
1:3 %>% map_dbl(~ 2 + .x)
```

```
## [1] 3 4 5
```

```
1:3 %>% map_dbl(~ 4 - .x)
```

```
## [1] 3 2 1
```

```
1:3 %>% map_dbl(~ .x - 4)
```

```
## [1] -3 -2 -1
```

Or you can use them for more readable versions of function composition.

```
1:3 %>% map_dbl(~ 3 * (.x + 2))
```

```
## [1] 9 12 15
```

If you need a lambda expression with two arguments, you can use .x and .y as the first and second argument, respectively.

```
map2_dbl(1:3, 1:3, ~ .x + .y)
```

```
## [1] 2 4 6
```

If you need more than two arguments, you can use .*n* for the *n*'th argument:

```
list(1:3, 1:3, 1:3) %>% pmap_dbl(~ .1 + .2 + .3)
```

```
## [1] 0.6 0.6 0.6
```

CHAPTER 7

Manipulating Data Frames: `dplyr`

The `dplyr` package resembles the functionality in the `purrr` package, but it is designed for manipulating data frames. It will be loaded with the `tidyverse` package, but you can also load it using

library(dplyr)

The usual way that you use `dplyr` is similar to how you use `purrr`. You string together a sequence of actions in a pipeline, with the actions separated by the %>% operator. The difference between the two packages is that the `purrr` functions work on sequences, while the `dplyr` functions work on data frames.

This package is huge and more functionality is added in each new release, so it would be impossible for me to describe everything you can do with `dplyr`. I can only give you a flavor of the package functionality and refer you to the documentation for more information.

Selecting Columns

One of the simplest operations you can do on a data frame is selecting one or more of its columns. You can do this by indexing with $:

```
iris_df <- as_tibble(iris)
print(iris_df, n = 3)
```

© Thomas Mailund 2019
T. Mailund, *R Data Science Quick Reference*, https://doi.org/10.1007/978-1-4842-4894-2_7

```
## # A tibble: 150 x 5
##    Sepal.Length Sepal.Width Petal.Length
##           <dbl>       <dbl>        <dbl>
## 1           5.1         3.5          1.4
## 2           4.9         3            1.4
## 3           4.7         3.2          1.3
## # ... with 147 more rows, and 2 more variables:
## #  Petal.Width <dbl>, Species <fct>
```

head(iris_df$Species)

```
## [1] setosa setosa setosa setosa setosa setosa
## Levels: setosa versicolor virginica
```

This, however, does not work well with pipelines where a data frame is flowing through from action to action. In dplyr, you have the function select() for picking out columns. You can give it one or more column names, and it will give you a data frame containing only those columns.

```
iris_df %>%
    select(Sepal.Length, Species) %>%
    print(n = 3)
```

```
## # A tibble: 150 x 2
##    Sepal.Length Species
##           <dbl> <fct>
## 1           5.1 setosa
## 2           4.9 setosa
## 3           4.7 setosa
## # ... with 147 more rows
```

You can also use complements when selecting columns; just put a minus in front of the column names.

```
iris_df %>%
    select(-Species) %>%
    print(n = 3)
```

```
## # A tibble: 150 x 4
##    Sepal.Length Sepal.Width Petal.Length
##           <dbl>       <dbl>        <dbl>
## 1          5.1         3.5          1.4
## 2          4.9         3            1.4
## 3          4.7         3.2          1.3
## # ... with 147 more rows, and 1 more variable:
## #   Petal.Width <dbl>
```

```
iris_df %>%
    select(-Species, -Sepal.Length) %>%
    print(n = 3)
```

```
## # A tibble: 150 x 3
##    Sepal.Width Petal.Length Petal.Width
##          <dbl>        <dbl>       <dbl>
## 1         3.5          1.4         0.2
## 2         3            1.4         0.2
## 3         3.2          1.3         0.2
## # ... with 147 more rows
```

You do not need to use column names. You can also use indices.

```
iris_df %>%
    select(1) %>%
    print(n = 3)
```

```
## # A tibble: 150 x 1
##    Sepal.Length
##           <dbl>
```

```
## 1            5.1
## 2            4.9
## 3            4.7
## # ... with 147 more rows
```

```
iris_df %>%
    select(1:3) %>%
    print(n = 3)
```

```
## # A tibble: 150 x 3
##    Sepal.Length Sepal.Width Petal.Length
##           <dbl>       <dbl>        <dbl>
## 1           5.1         3.5          1.4
## 2           4.9         3            1.4
## 3           4.7         3.2          1.3
## # ... with 147 more rows
```

This, of course, is less informative about what is being selected when you read the code. The second selection in the preceding code shows that you can extract ranges. You can also do this with column names.

```
iris_df %>%
    select(Petal.Length:Species) %>%
    print(n = 3)
```

```
## # A tibble: 150 x 3
##    Petal.Length Petal.Width Species
##           <dbl>       <dbl> <fct>
## 1           1.4         0.2 setosa
## 2           1.4         0.2 setosa
## 3           1.3         0.2 setosa
## # ... with 147 more rows
```

With `select()` you can also use various predicates for selecting columns. For example, you can pick columns based on the properties of the names. The `starts_with()` function lets you select columns based on the prefix of the column names and the `ends_with()` function based on the suffix of the column names:

```
iris_df %>%
    select(starts_with("Petal")) %>%
    print(n = 3)
```

```
## # A tibble: 150 x 2
##    Petal.Length Petal.Width
##           <dbl>       <dbl>
## 1           1.4         0.2
## 2           1.4         0.2
## 3           1.3         0.2
## # ... with 147 more rows
```

```
iris_df %>%
    select(-starts_with("Petal")) %>%
    print(n = 3)
```

```
## # A tibble: 150 x 3
##    Sepal.Length Sepal.Width Species
##           <dbl>       <dbl> <fct>
## 1           5.1         3.5 setosa
## 2           4.9         3   setosa
## 3           4.7         3.2 setosa
## # ... with 147 more rows
```

```
iris_df %>%
    select(starts_with("Petal"), Species) %>%
    print(n = 3)
```

```
## # A tibble: 150 x 3
##    Petal.Length Petal.Width Species
##           <dbl>       <dbl> <fct>
## 1           1.4         0.2 setosa
## 2           1.4         0.2 setosa
## 3           1.3         0.2 setosa
## # ... with 147 more rows
```

```
iris_df %>%
    select(starts_with("PETAL", ignore.case = TRUE)) %>%
    print(n = 3)
```

```
## # A tibble: 150 x 2
##    Petal.Length Petal.Width
##           <dbl>       <dbl>
## 1           1.4         0.2
## 2           1.4         0.2
## 3           1.3         0.2
## # ... with 147 more rows
```

```
iris_df %>%
    select(starts_with("S")) %>%
    print(n = 3)
```

```
## # A tibble: 150 x 3
##    Sepal.Length Sepal.Width Species
##           <dbl>       <dbl> <fct>
## 1           5.1         3.5 setosa
## 2           4.9         3   setosa
## 3           4.7         3.2 setosa
## # ... with 147 more rows
```

```
iris_df %>%
    select(ends_with("Length")) %>%
    print(n = 3)
```

```
## # A tibble: 150 x 2
##    Sepal.Length Petal.Length
##           <dbl>        <dbl>
## 1           5.1          1.4
## 2           4.9          1.4
## 3           4.7          1.3
## # ... with 147 more rows
```

If you use the `contains()` function, you select columns whose names contain a string.

```
iris_df %>%
    select(contains("ng")) %>%
    print(n = 3)
```

```
## # A tibble: 150 x 2
##    Sepal.Length Petal.Length
##           <dbl>        <dbl>
## 1           5.1          1.4
## 2           4.9          1.4
## 3           4.7          1.3
## # ... with 147 more rows
```

The most powerful predicate function is `matches()`. It lets you select columns using regular expressions. For the `iris_df` example, there is not much that you can select using a regular expression that you cannot select using one of the simpler functions, but consider this table:

```
df <- tribble(
    ~a1x, ~ax, ~a2x, ~b2, ~b2y, ~by,
    1, 2, 3, 4, 5, 6
)
```

We can pick a column that contains an integer using the regular expression .*\\d.*:

```
df %>%
    select(matches(".*\\d.*")) %>%
    print(n = 3)

## # A tibble: 1 x 4
##     a1x   a2x    b2   b2y
##   <dbl> <dbl> <dbl> <dbl>
## 1     1     3     4     5
```

If we need the names to have non-empty strings before and after the digit, we can use this expression:

```
df %>%
    select(matches(".+\\d.+")) %>%
    print(n = 3)

## # A tibble: 1 x 3
##     a1x   a2x   b2y
##   <dbl> <dbl> <dbl>
## 1     1     3     5
```

You can also use select() to rename columns. If you use a named parameter, the columns you select will get the names you use for the function parameters.

```
iris_df %>%
    select(sepal_length = Sepal.Length,
           sepal_width = Sepal.Width) %>%
    print(n = 3)

## # A tibble: 150 x 2
##    sepal_length sepal_width
##           <dbl>       <dbl>
```

```
## 1          5.1        3.5
## 2          4.9        3
## 3          4.7        3.2
## # ... with 147 more rows
```

Since select() removes the columns you do *not* select, it might not always be the best approach. A similar function to select(), where you do not lose columns, is rename(). With this function, you can rename columns and keep the remaining columns as well.

```
iris_df %>%
    rename(sepal_length = Sepal.Length,
           sepal_width = Sepal.Width) %>%
    print(n = 3)
```

```
## # A tibble: 150 x 5
##   sepal_length sepal_width Petal.Length
##          <dbl>       <dbl>        <dbl>
## 1          5.1         3.5          1.4
## 2          4.9         3            1.4
## 3          4.7         3.2          1.3
## # ... with 147 more rows, and 2 more variables:
## #  Petal.Width <dbl>, Species <fct>
```

Filter

While select() extracts a subset of columns, the filter() function does the same for rows.

The iris_df contains three different species. We can see this using the distinct() function. This function is also from the dplyr package, and it gives you all the unique rows from selected columns.

```
iris_df %>%
    distinct(Species)
```

```
## # A tibble: 3 x 1
##   Species
##   <fct>
## 1 setosa
## 2 versicolor
## 3 virginica
```

We can select the rows where the species is "setosa" using filter():

```
iris_df %>%
    filter(Species == "setosa") %>%
    print(n = 3)
```

```
## # A tibble: 50 x 5
##   Sepal.Length Sepal.Width Petal.Length
##          <dbl>       <dbl>        <dbl>
## 1          5.1         3.5          1.4
## 2          4.9         3            1.4
## 3          4.7         3.2          1.3
## # ... with 47 more rows, and 2 more variables:
## #   Petal.Width <dbl>, Species <fct>
```

We can combine filter() and select() in a pipeline to get a subset of the columns as well as a subset of the rows.

```
iris_df %>%
    filter(Species == "setosa") %>%
    select(ends_with("Length"), Species) %>%
    print(n = 3)
```

```
## # A tibble: 50 x 3
##   Sepal.Length Petal.Length Species
```

```
##             <dbl>        <dbl> <fct>
## 1            5.1          1.4 setosa
## 2            4.9          1.4 setosa
## 3            4.7          1.3 setosa
## # ... with 47 more rows
```

Generally, we can string together as many dplyr (or purrr) functions as we desire in pipelines.

```
iris_df %>%
    filter(Species != "setosa") %>%
    distinct(Species) %>%
    print(n = 3)
```

```
## # A tibble: 2 x 1
##   Species
##   <fct>
## 1 versicolor
## 2 virginica
```

We can use more than one columns to filter by

```
iris_df %>%
    filter(Sepal.Length > 5, Petal.Width < 0.4) %>%
    print(n = 3)
```

```
## # A tibble: 15 x 5
##   Sepal.Length Sepal.Width Petal.Length
##          <dbl>       <dbl>        <dbl>
## 1          5.1         3.5          1.4
## 2          5.4         3.7          1.5
## 3          5.8         4            1.2
## # ... with 12 more rows, and 2 more variables:
## #  Petal.Width <dbl>, Species <fct>
```

We can also use functions as a predicate, for example, the between() function to select numbers in a given range.

```
iris_df %>%
    filter(between(Sepal.Width, 2, 2.5)) %>%
    print(n = 3)

## # A tibble: 19 x 5
##   Sepal.Length Sepal.Width Petal.Length
##          <dbl>       <dbl>        <dbl>
## 1          4.5         2.3          1.3
## 2          5.5         2.3          4
## 3          4.9         2.4          3.3
## # ... with 16 more rows, and 2 more variables:
## #   Petal.Width <dbl>, Species <fct>
```

We cannot use the functions starts_with(), ends_with(), and so on. that we can use with select(). This does not mean, however, that we cannot filter rows using string patterns. We just need different functions. For example, we can use str_starts() from the stringr package. We return to stringr in Chapter 8.

```
iris_df %>%
    filter(str_starts(Species, "v")) %>%
    print(n = 3)

## # A tibble: 100 x 5
##   Sepal.Length Sepal.Width Petal.Length
##          <dbl>       <dbl>        <dbl>
## 1          7            3.2          4.7
## 2          6.4          3.2          4.5
## 3          6.9          3.1          4.9
## # ... with 97 more rows, and 2 more variables:
## #   Petal.Width <dbl>, Species <fct>
```

```
iris_df %>%
    filter(str_ends(Species, "r")) %>%
    print(n = 3)
```

```
## # A tibble: 50 x 5
##    Sepal.Length Sepal.Width Petal.Length
##           <dbl>       <dbl>        <dbl>
## 1             7         3.2          4.7
## 2           6.4         3.2          4.5
## 3           6.9         3.1          4.9
## # ... with 47 more rows, and 2 more variables:
## #   Petal.Width <dbl>, Species <fct>
```

While filter() selects rows by applying predicates on individual columns, other filter variants will use predicates over more than one column.

The filter_all() function will apply the predicate over all columns. You must provide an expression where you use . (dot) for the table cell value and wrap the expression in one of two functions: any_var() or all_var(). If you use any_var(), it suffices that one column satisfies the predicate for the row to be included; if you use all_var(), then all columns must satisfy the predicate.

We can require that any value in the iris_df data must be larger than five:

```
iris_df %>%
    select(-Species) %>%
    filter_all(any_vars(. > 5)) %>%
    print(n = 3)
```

```
## # A tibble: 118 x 4
##    Sepal.Length Sepal.Width Petal.Length
##           <dbl>       <dbl>        <dbl>
## 1           5.1         3.5          1.4
## 2           5.4         3.9          1.7
## 3           5.4         3.7          1.5
## # ... with 115 more rows, and 1 more variable:
## #   Petal.Width <dbl>
```

The expression . > 5 is not meaningful if . is a string, so I had to remove the Species column before I filtered. Rarely will we accept to lose an informative variable. If you want to keep a column, but not apply the predicate to values in it, you can use the filter_at() function.

```
iris_df %>%
    filter_at(vars(-Species), any_vars(. > 5)) %>%
    print(n = 3)
```

```
## # A tibble: 118 x 5
##    Sepal.Length Sepal.Width Petal.Length
##           <dbl>       <dbl>        <dbl>
## 1           5.1         3.5          1.4
## 2           5.4         3.9          1.7
## 3           5.4         3.7          1.5
## # ... with 115 more rows, and 2 more variables:
## #   Petal.Width <dbl>, Species <fct>
```

You can give filter_at() a vector of strings or a vector of variables (unquoted column names). Because I need to negate Species to select all other columns, I used vars() here. In other cases, you can use either option.

```
iris_df %>%
    filter_at(c("Petal.Length", "Sepal.Length"),
              any_vars(. > 0)) %>%
    print(n = 3)
```

```
## # A tibble: 150 x 5
##    Sepal.Length Sepal.Width Petal.Length
##           <dbl>       <dbl>        <dbl>
## 1          5.1         3.5          1.4
## 2          4.9         3            1.4
## 3          4.7         3.2          1.3
## # ... with 147 more rows, and 2 more variables:
## #   Petal.Width <dbl>, Species <fct>
```

```
iris_df %>%
    filter_at(vars(Petal.Length, Sepal.Length),
              any_vars(. > 0)) %>%
    print(n = 3)
```

```
## # A tibble: 150 x 5
##    Sepal.Length Sepal.Width Petal.Length
##           <dbl>       <dbl>        <dbl>
## 1          5.1         3.5          1.4
## 2          4.9         3            1.4
## 3          4.7         3.2          1.3
## # ... with 147 more rows, and 2 more variables:
## #   Petal.Width <dbl>, Species <fct>
```

You can use filter_if() to use a predicate over the columns:

```
iris_df %>%
    filter_if(is.numeric, all_vars(. < 5)) %>%
    print(n = 3)
```

```
## # A tibble: 22 x 5
##    Sepal.Length Sepal.Width Petal.Length
##           <dbl>       <dbl>        <dbl>
## 1           4.9           3          1.4
## 2           4.7         3.2          1.3
## 3           4.6         3.1          1.5
## # ... with 19 more rows, and 2 more variables:
## #   Petal.Width <dbl>, Species <fct>
```

You can use functions or lambda expressions as the predicate.

Consider a case where we have numbers with missing data in a table. If we want to filter the rows where all values are greater than three, we can use filter_all():

```
df <- tribble(
    ~A, ~B, ~C,
     1,  2,  3,
     4,  5, NA,
    11, 12, 13,
    22, 22,  1
)
df %>% filter_all(all_vars(. > 3))
```

```
## # A tibble: 1 x 3
##        A     B     C
##    <dbl> <dbl> <dbl>
## 1     11    12    13
```

It removes the first two and the last row because they all contain values smaller or equal to three. It also deletes the third row because NA is not considered greater than three. We can restrict the tests to the columns that do not contain missing values:

```
df %>%
    filter_if(~ all(!is.na(.)), all_vars(. > 3))
```

```
## # A tibble: 3 x 3
##       A     B     C
##    <dbl> <dbl> <dbl>
## 1     4     5    NA
## 2    11    12    13
## 3    22    22     1
```

This removes column C from the tests. It means that we also keep the last row even though C has a value smaller than three.

If you want to keep the two middle row but not the first or last, you can write a more complex predicate and use filter_all().

```
df %>% filter_all(all_vars(is.na(.) | . > 3))
```

```
## # A tibble: 2 x 3
##       A     B     C
##    <dbl> <dbl> <dbl>
## 1     4     5    NA
## 2    11    12    13
```

You need to use the | vector-or. The expression needs to be a vector expression so you cannot use ||.

Many dplyr functions have _all, _at, and _if variants, but I will only describe the frequently used functions here. For the others, I refer to the package documentation.

Sorting

If you want to sort rows by values in selected columns, the function you want is called arrange(). You can sort by one or more columns:

```
iris_df %>%
    arrange(Petal.Length) %>%
    print(n = 5)
```

125

```
## # A tibble: 150 x 5
##    Sepal.Length Sepal.Width Petal.Length
##           <dbl>       <dbl>        <dbl>
## 1          4.6         3.6            1
## 2          4.3         3            1.1
## 3          5.8         4            1.2
## 4          5           3.2          1.2
## 5          4.7         3.2          1.3
## # ... with 145 more rows, and 2 more variables:
## #  Petal.Width <dbl>, Species <fct>
```

```
iris_df %>%
    arrange(Sepal.Length, Petal.Length) %>%
    print(n = 5)
```

```
## # A tibble: 150 x 5
##    Sepal.Length Sepal.Width Petal.Length
##           <dbl>       <dbl>        <dbl>
## 1          4.3         3            1.1
## 2          4.4         3            1.3
## 3          4.4         3.2          1.3
## 4          4.4         2.9          1.4
## 5          4.5         2.3          1.3
## # ... with 145 more rows, and 2 more variables:
## #  Petal.Width <dbl>, Species <fct>
```

If you want to sort in descending order, you can use the function desc().

```
iris_df %>%
    arrange(desc(Petal.Length)) %>%
    print(n = 5)
```

```
## # A tibble: 150 x 5
##    Sepal.Length Sepal.Width Petal.Length
##           <dbl>       <dbl>        <dbl>
## 1          7.7         2.6          6.9
## 2          7.7         3.8          6.7
## 3          7.7         2.8          6.7
## 4          7.6         3            6.6
## 5          7.9         3.8          6.4
## # ... with 145 more rows, and 2 more variables:
## #   Petal.Width <dbl>, Species <fct>
```

Modifying Data Frames

When we work with data frames, we usually want to compute values based on the variables (columns) in our tables. Filtering rows and columns will only get us so far.

The mutate() function lets us add columns to a data frame based on expressions that can involve any of the existing columns. Consider a table of widths and heights.

```
df <- tribble(
    ~height, ~width,
        10,     12,
        42,     24,
        14,     12
)
```

We can add an area column using mutate() and this expression:

```
df %>% mutate(area = height * width)
```

```
## # A tibble: 3 x 3
##    height width   area
```

```
##      <dbl> <dbl> <dbl>
## 1      10    12   120
## 2      42    24  1008
## 3      14    12   168
```

If you add columns to a data frame, you can refer to variables you have already added. For example, if your height and width data are in inches and you want them in centimeters, and you also want the area in centimeters squared, you can do this:

```
cm_per_inch = 2.54
df %>% mutate(
    height_cm = cm_per_inch * height,
    width_cm = cm_per_inch * width,
    area_cm = height_cm * width_cm
)
```

```
## # A tibble: 3 x 5
##    height width height_cm width_cm area_cm
##     <dbl> <dbl>     <dbl>    <dbl>   <dbl>
## 1      10    12      25.4     30.5    774.
## 2      42    24     107.      61.0   6503.
## 3      14    12      35.6     30.5   1084.
```

The following expression, however, will not work since you cannot refer to variables you are adding later in the mutate() call.

```
df %>% mutate(
    area_cm   = height_cm * width_cm,
    height_cm = cm_per_inch * height,
    width_cm  = cm_per_inch * width
)
```

If you do not give the new variable a name, that is, you call `mutate()` with named parameters, then the expression will become the variable name:

```
df %>% mutate(cm_per_inch * height)
```

```
## # A tibble: 3 x 3
##    height width `cm_per_inch * height`
##     <dbl> <dbl>                  <dbl>
## 1      10    12                   25.4
## 2      42    24                  107.
## 3      14    12                   35.6
```

In this example, the units (inches and centimeters), are not encoded with the data, and in future computations, you might end up mixing the wrong units. If you use the `units` package—which is not part of the Tidyverse—you can make the units explicit, automatically convert between units where that makes sense, and you will get unit type safety as a bonus.

```
library(units)
```

```
df %>% mutate(
    height_in = units::as_units(height, "in"),
    width_in  = units::as_units(width, "in"),
    area_in   = height_in * width_in,
    height_cm = units::set_units(height_in, "cm"),
    width_cm  = units::set_units(width_in, "cm"),
    area_cm   = units::set_units(area_in, "cm^2")
)
```

```
## # A tibble: 3 x 8
##    height width height_in width_in area_in
##     <dbl> <dbl>      [in]     [in]  [in^2]
## 1      10    12        10       12     120
## 2      42    24        42       24    1008
```

```
## 3      14     12          14        12      168
## # ... with 3 more variables: height_cm [cm],
## #   width_cm [cm], area_cm [cm^2]
```

This is possible because tibbles can contain classes of various types, which the units package exploits. Tibbles use an interface that lets you define how your own classes should be displayed,[1] but this is beyond the scope of this book.

In the preceding example, we created unit-carrying values for the original data table, but the original height and weight columns are still around. We could use select() to remove them, but the function transmute() already does this for us.

```
df %>% transmute(
    height_in = units::as_units(height, "in"),
    width_in  = units::as_units(width, "in"),
    area_in   = height_in * width_in,
    height_cm = units::set_units(height_in, "cm"),
    width_cm  = units::set_units(width_in, "cm"),
    area_cm   = units::set_units(area_in, "cm^2")
)
```

```
## # A tibble: 3 x 6
##   height_in width_in area_in height_cm width_cm
##        [in]     [in]  [in^2]      [cm]     [cm]
## 1        10       12     120     25.40    30.48
## 2        42       24    1008    106.68    60.96
## 3        14       12     168     35.56    30.48
## # ... with 1 more variable: area_cm [cm^2]
```

---

[1]http://tinyurl.com/yya2btby

130

When you use `transmute()` instead of `mutate()`, the variables that you are not assigning to will be removed.

As with filtering, the expressions you use when mutating a data frame must be vector expressions. Consider this example:

```
df <- tibble(
    x = rnorm(3, mean = 12, sd = 5),
)
my_abs <- function(x) if (x < 0) -x else x
df %>% mutate(my_abs(x))

## Warning in if (x < 0) -x else x: the condition has
## length > 1 and only the first element will be used

## # A tibble: 3 x 2
##        x `my_abs(x)`
##    <dbl>       <dbl>
## 1 16.1        16.1
## 2 -2.07       -2.07
## 3 14.9        14.9
```

It fails because the function `my_abs()` (my version of the `abs()` function) is not a vector expression. It is not a vector expression because of x in the `if` expression.

If we use the built-in `abs()` function, then there is no problem with the expression; it handles vectors.

```
df %>% mutate(abs(x))

## # A tibble: 3 x 2
##        x `abs(x)`
##    <dbl>    <dbl>
## 1 16.1     16.1
## 2 -2.07     2.07
## 3 14.9     14.9
```

If you use the ifelse() vector version of if expressions, you get a vector expression.

```
ifelse_abs <- function(x) ifelse(x < 0, -x, x)
df %>% mutate(ifelse_abs(x))
```

```
## # A tibble: 3 x 2
##        x `ifelse_abs(x)`
##    <dbl>          <dbl>
## 1 16.1           16.1
## 2 -2.07           2.07
## 3 14.9           14.9
```

Or you can use the Vectorize() function to make a vector expression out of a function that does not handle vectors.

```
my_abs <- Vectorize(my_abs)
df %>% mutate(my_abs(x))
```

```
## # A tibble: 3 x 2
##        x `my_abs(x)`
##    <dbl>      <dbl>
## 1 16.1       16.1
## 2 -2.07       2.07
## 3 14.9       14.9
```

If you need to map the input to several different output values, you can nest ifelse() expressions arbitrarily deep, but it gets difficult to read. A function that alleviates this problem substantially is case_when(). You can give it a sequence of predicates with matching expressions, and it will return the expression for the first matching predicate.

Consider this example where we use case_when() to categorize the variable x based on its value:

```
df <- tibble(x = rnorm(100))
df %>%
    mutate(
        x_category = case_when(
            x - mean(x) < -2 * sd(x) ~ "small",
            x - mean(x) > 2 * sd(x) ~ "large",
            TRUE ~ "medium"
        )
    ) %>%
    print(n = 3)

## # A tibble: 100 x 2
##          x x_category
##      <dbl> <chr>
## 1 -0.311   medium
## 2  0.0992  medium
## 3 -1.26    medium
## # ... with 97 more rows
```

The TRUE line corresponds to the else part of an if-else statement.

Grouping and Summarizing

In many analyses, we need summary statistics of our data. If you can map one or more of your columns into a single summary, you can use the summarise() function.

```
df <- tibble(x = rnorm(100), y = rnorm(100))
df %>% summarise(mean_x = mean(x), mean_y = mean(y))
```

```
## # A tibble: 1 x 2
##     mean_x mean_y
##      <dbl>  <dbl>
## 1 -0.0529 0.0141
```

In this example, we summarized our data as the mean of variables x and y.

If you split your data into different classes and want to work on the data per group, you can use the function group_by().

```
classify <- function(x) {
    case_when(
        x - mean(x) < -2 * sd(x) ~ "small",
        x - mean(x) > 2 * sd(x) ~ "large",
        TRUE ~ "medium"
    )
}
df %>%
    mutate(x_category = classify(x)) %>%
    group_by(x_category) %>%
    print(n = 3)
```

```
## # A tibble: 100 x 3
## # Groups: x_category [2]
##        x     y x_category
##    <dbl> <dbl> <chr>
## 1 -0.702 0.959 medium
## 2  1.10  0.557 medium
## 3 -0.667 0.399 medium
## # ... with 97 more rows
```

The result is a data frame that, when we print it, doesn't look different from before we grouped the data.

```
df %>%
    mutate(x_category = classify(x)) %>%
    print(n = 3)
## # A tibble: 100 x 3
##         x     y x_category
##     <dbl> <dbl> <chr>
## 1 -0.702 0.959 medium
## 2  1.10  0.557 medium
## 3 -0.667 0.399 medium
## # ... with 97 more rows
```

In the header, however, you will notice the line

```
# Groups:   x_category [3]
```

This tells you that something *is* different when you have grouped your data. This is apparent when you combine grouping with summarizing.

```
df %>%
    mutate(x_category = classify(x)) %>%
    group_by(x_category) %>%
    summarise(mean_x = mean(x), no_x = n())
## # A tibble: 2 x 3
##    x_category mean_x  no_x
##    <chr>       <dbl> <int>
## 1 large        2.34     4
## 2 medium      -0.153   96
```

When you group your data and then summarize, you get a per-group summary statistics. Here, we calculate the mean and the number of observations in each category (the function n() gives you the number of observations).

You can get the variables your data is grouped by using the group_vars() function.

```
df %>%
    mutate(x_category = classify(x)) %>%
    group_by(x_category) %>%
    group_vars()
```

```
## [1] "x_category"
```

You can group data by more than one variable.

```
df <- tibble(x = rnorm(100), y = rnorm(100))
df %>%
    mutate(
        x_category = classify(x),
        y_category = classify(y)
    ) %>%
    group_by(x_category, y_category) %>%
    group_vars()
```

```
## [1] "x_category" "y_category"
```

If you do, you will get summaries for each combination of the grouping variables.

```
df %>%
    mutate(
        x_category = classify(x),
        y_category = classify(y)
    ) %>%
    group_by(x_category, y_category) %>%
    summarise(mean_x = mean(x), mean_y = mean(y))
```

```
## # A tibble: 6 x 4
```

```
## # Groups:    x_category [3]
##    x_category y_category mean_x   mean_y
##    <chr>      <chr>       <dbl>    <dbl>
## 1 large      medium       2.02   -0.836
## 2 medium     large        0.871   1.98
## 3 medium     medium      -0.118   0.0213
## 4 medium     small       -0.679  -2.69
## 5 small      large       -3.48    1.96
## 6 small      medium      -2.74   -0.0693
```

If you group by one variable and summarize another, you get summaries for both variables according for each of the *grouped by* variables.

```
df %>%
    mutate(
        x_category = classify(x),
        y_category = classify(y)
    ) %>%
    group_by(x_category) %>%
    summarise(mean_x = mean(x), mean_y = mean(y))
```

```
## # A tibble: 3 x 3
##    x_category mean_x   mean_y
##    <chr>       <dbl>    <dbl>
## 1 large        2.02   -0.836
## 2 medium      -0.114   0.0133
## 3 small       -2.98    0.607
```

Here, we calculate the mean of x and y for each category of x value. In general, you can use any number of variables to group the data and any number of variables to summarize, and the summaries will be computed per group.

When you have grouped your data by more than one variable, a summary will remove the last group you added, that is, the last variable you grouped by. A summary gives you a new data frame containing the grouping variable and the summaries. If you have grouped with more than one variable, this data frame will be grouped by all but the last grouping variables.

For example, if we group by variables A and B and then summarise another variable, C, the result will be grouped by A and not B. If you group by A, B, and D, the result will be a data frame grouped by A and B.

```
df2 <- tribble(
    ~A,        ~B,       ~C, ~D,
    "left",   "up",      2, "yes",
    "right",  "up",      5, "no",
    "left",   "down",    2, "yes",
    "left",   "down",    7, "no",
    "left",   "down",    3, "no",
    "right",  "up",      8, "yes",
    "right",  "up",      2, "yes",
    "right",  "up",      8, "no"
)
df2 %>% group_by(A, B) %>%
    summarise(min_c = min(C), max_c = max(C))

## # A tibble: 3 x 4
## # Groups:    A [2]
##    A      B      min_c max_c
##    <chr>  <chr>  <dbl> <dbl>
## 1 left   down       2     7
## 2 left   up         2     2
## 3 right  up         2     8
```

```
df2 %>% group_by(A, B) %>%
    summarise(min_c = min(C), max_c = max(C)) %>%
    summarise(max_diff = max(max_c - min_c))
```

```
## # A tibble: 2 x 2
##   A       max_diff
##   <chr>      <dbl>
## 1 left           5
## 2 right          6
```

```
df2 %>% group_by(A, B, D) %>%
    summarise(min_c = min(C), max_c = max(C))
```

```
## # A tibble: 5 x 5
## # Groups:   A, B [3]
##   A     B     D     min_c max_c
##   <chr> <chr> <chr> <dbl> <dbl>
## 1 left  down  no        3     7
## 2 left  down  yes       2     2
## 3 left  up    yes       2     2
## 4 right up    no        5     8
## 5 right up    yes       2     8
```

```
df2 %>% group_by(A, B, D) %>%
    summarise(min_c = min(C), max_c = max(C)) %>%
    summarise(max_diff = max(max_c - min_c))
```

```
## # A tibble: 3 x 3
## # Groups:   A [2]
##   A     B     max_diff
##   <chr> <chr>    <dbl>
## 1 left  down         4
## 2 left  up           0
## 3 right up           6
```

The order you use in group_by() is important here. If you flip the variables, you will get a data frame that is still grouped by B instead.

```
df2 %>% group_by(A, B) %>%
    summarise(min_c = min(C), max_c = max(C))
```

```
## # A tibble: 3 x 4
## # Groups:   A [2]
##    A     B     min_c max_c
##    <chr> <chr> <dbl> <dbl>
## 1 left  down      2     7
## 2 left  up        2     2
## 3 right up        2     8
```

The way grouping variables are removed one by one each time you call summarise() is a potential source of errors. Say you have variables A, B, C, and D, grouped by A, B, and D. Within each combination of these, you define a distance as the maximum value of C minus its minimum value. You want to know the smallest difference between maximum and minimum in the overall data. You might, reasonably, try this:

You compute the minimum and maximum per group:

```
df2 %>% group_by(A, B, D) %>%
    summarise(min_c = min(C), max_c = max(C)) %>%
```

```
## Error: <text>:3:0: unexpected end of input
## 1: df2 %>% group_by(A, B, D) %>%
## 2:     summarise(min_c = min(C), max_c = max(C)) %>%
##    ^
```

Then you try another summarise() to find the minimum between max_c and min_c for each row in the result:

```
df2 %>% group_by(A, B, D) %>%
    summarise(min_c = min(C), max_c = max(C)) %>%
    summarise(min_diff = min(max_c - min_c))
```

```
## # A tibble: 3 x 3
## # Groups:    A [2]
##    A     B      min_diff
##    <chr> <chr>     <dbl>
## 1 left  down          0
## 2 left  up            0
## 3 right up            3
```

This, however, gives you the smallest difference for each combination of A and B, but not the overall smallest. The first summarise only removes the D group (and the second removes B).

If you have grouped your data, or you get grouped data from one summary as in the preceding example, you can remove the groups again using ungroup(). Once you have done this, you can compute global summaries again.

```
df2 %>% group_by(A, B, D) %>%
    summarise(min_c = min(C), max_c = max(C)) %>%
    ungroup() %>%
    summarise(min_diff = min(max_c - min_c))
```

```
## # A tibble: 1 x 1
##    min_diff
##       <dbl>
## 1         0
```

Grouping is not only useful when collecting summaries of your data. You can also add columns to your data frame based on per-group computations using mutate():

```
df %>%
    mutate(
        x_category = classify(x),
        y_category = classify(y)
    ) %>%
```

```
    group_by(x_category) %>%
    mutate(mean_x = mean(x), mean_y = mean(y)) %>%
    print(n = 5)
```

```
## # A tibble: 100 x 6
## # Groups:   x_category [3]
##         x        y x_category y_category mean_x
##     <dbl>    <dbl> <chr>      <chr>       <dbl>
## 1   0.352   1.23   medium     medium     -0.114
## 2  -2.84   -0.705  small      medium     -2.98
## 3   0.332  -0.0964 medium     medium     -0.114
## 4   1.37   -1.28   medium     medium     -0.114
## 5  -0.893  -0.373  medium     medium     -0.114
## # ... with 95 more rows, and 1 more variable:
## #   mean_y <dbl>
```

When you calculate a summary and then mutate, you create columns where a summary parameter takes values based on the groupings, but they are combined with the existing data rather than extracted as a new data frame as summarise() would do.

A mutate() without a group_by() will give you summaries for the entire data.

```
df %>%
    mutate(
        x_category = classify(x),
        y_category = classify(y)
    ) %>%
    mutate(mean_x = mean(x), mean_y = mean(y))
```

```
## # A tibble: 100 x 6
##          x        y x_category y_category mean_x
##      <dbl>    <dbl> <chr>      <chr>       <dbl>
##  1  0.352   1.23    medium     medium     -0.157
##  2 -2.84   -0.705   small      medium     -0.157
##  3  0.332  -0.0964  medium     medium     -0.157
##  4  1.37   -1.28    medium     medium     -0.157
##  5 -0.893  -0.373   medium     medium     -0.157
##  6 -0.561   0.465   medium     medium     -0.157
##  7 -1.14   -0.874   medium     medium     -0.157
##  8  0.812  -0.897   medium     medium     -0.157
##  9  0.162   0.634   medium     medium     -0.157
## 10 -1.12   -0.311   medium     medium     -0.157
## # ... with 90 more rows, and 1 more variable:
## #   mean_y <dbl>
```

In contrast, if you group before adding variables to the data, then the summaries are per group.

```
df %>%
    mutate(
        x_category = classify(x),
        y_category = classify(y)
    ) %>%
    group_by(x_category) %>%
    mutate(mean_x = mean(x), mean_y = mean(y))
```

```
## # A tibble: 100 x 6
## # Groups:   x_category [3]
##          x        y x_category y_category mean_x
##      <dbl>    <dbl> <chr>      <chr>       <dbl>
##  1  0.352   1.23    medium     medium     -0.114
##  2 -2.84   -0.705   small      medium     -2.98
```

```
##  3  0.332 -0.0964 medium        medium        -0.114
##  4  1.37  -1.28   medium        medium        -0.114
##  5 -0.893 -0.373  medium        medium        -0.114
##  6 -0.561  0.465  medium        medium        -0.114
##  7 -1.14  -0.874  medium        medium        -0.114
##  8  0.812 -0.897  medium        medium        -0.114
##  9  0.162  0.634  medium        medium        -0.114
## 10 -1.12  -0.311  medium        medium        -0.114
## # ...  with 90 more rows, and 1 more variable:
## #  mean_y <dbl>
```

You can combine data-wide summaries with grouped summaries if you calculate the global summaries before you group.

```
df %>%
    mutate(
        x_category = classify(x),
        y_category = classify(y)
    ) %>%
    mutate(mean_y = mean(y)) %>%
    group_by(x_category) %>%
    mutate(mean_x = mean(x)) %>%
    distinct(mean_x, mean_y)

## # A tibble: 3 x 3
## # Groups:   x_category [3]
##   mean_x mean_y x_category
##    <dbl>  <dbl> <chr>
## 1 -0.114 0.0142 medium
## 2 -2.98  0.0142 small
## 3  2.02  0.0142 large
```

Here I used mutate() + distinct() rather than summarise() to keep all the variables in the output. With summarise(), I would only keep the grouping variables and the summaries.

If you need to compute summaries with different groups, for example, the mean for x for each x_category as well as the mean of y for each y_category, then you can call group_by(x_category) for summarizing x, followed by group_by(y_category) for changing the grouping so you can summarize y.

```
df %>%
    mutate(
        x_category = classify(x),
        y_category = classify(y)
    ) %>%
    group_by(x_category) %>%
    mutate(mean_x = mean(x)) %>%
    group_by(y_category) %>%
    mutate(mean_y = mean(y)) %>%
    distinct(
        x_category, mean_x,
        y_category, mean_y
    )

## # A tibble: 6 x 4
## # Groups:   y_category [3]
##   x_category mean_x y_category  mean_y
##   <chr>       <dbl> <chr>        <dbl>
## 1 medium     -0.114 medium     0.00175
## 2 small      -2.98  medium     0.00175
## 3 medium     -0.114 large      1.97
## 4 medium     -0.114 small      -2.69
## 5 small      -2.98  large      1.97
## 6 large       2.02  medium     0.00175
```

Joining Tables

It is not uncommon to have your data in more than one table. This could be because the tables are created from different calculations, for example, different kinds of summaries, or it can be because you got the data from different files.

If you merely need to combine tables by row or column, then you can use the bind_rows() and bind_columns() functions which do precisely what you would expect.

```
df1 <- tibble(
    A = paste0("a", 1:2),
    B = paste0("b", 1:2)
)
df2 <- tibble(
    A = paste0("a", 3:4),
    B = paste0("b", 3:4)
)
df3 <- tibble(
    C = paste0("c", 1:2),
    D = paste0("d", 1:2)
)
bind_rows(df1, df2)

## # A tibble: 4 x 2
##    A     B
##    <chr> <chr>
## 1 a1    b1
## 2 a2    b2
## 3 a3    b3
## 4 a4    b4
```

```
bind_cols(df1, df3)
```

```
## # A tibble: 2 x 4
##    A     B     C     D
##    <chr> <chr> <chr> <chr>
## 1 a1    b1    c1    d1
## 2 a2    b2    c2    d2
```

When you combine rows, the tables must have the same columns, and when you combine by column, the tables must have the same number of rows.

If you have tables that represent different relations between variables—the underlying principle of relational databases aimed at avoiding duplicated data—then you can combine them using join functions.

Say you have a table that maps students to grades for each class you teach. You can join tables from two different classes using inner_join(). You use a key to join them on, specified by argument by.

```
grades_maths <- tribble(
    ~name,              ~grade,
    "Marko Polo",       "D",
    "Isaac Newton",     "A+",
    "Charles Darwin",   "B"
)
grades_biology <- tribble(
    ~name,              ~grade,
    "Marko Polo",       "F",
    "Isaac Newton",     "D",
    "Charles Darwin",   "A+"
)
```

```
inner_join(grades_maths, grades_biology, by = "name")
```

```
## # A tibble: 3 x 3
##    name            grade.x grade.y
##    <chr>           <chr>   <chr>
## 1 Marko Polo       D       F
## 2 Isaac Newton     A+      D
## 3 Charles Darwin   B       A+
```

This tells inner_join() that you want to combine all rows in the first table with all rows in the second, where the two rows have the same name. You can use more than one key in a join if you give by a vector of variable names.

In the previous example, each name appears once per table. If a key appears more than once, then the result of an inner join will have a list with all combinations of rows sharing a name.

```
grades_maths2 <- tribble(
    ~name,               ~grade,
    "Marko Polo",        "D",
    "Isaac Newton",      "A+", # so good at physics
    "Isaac Newton",      "A+", # that he got an A+ twice
    "Charles Darwin",    "B"
)
grades_biology2 <- tribble(
    ~name,               ~grade,
    "Marko Polo",        "F",
    "Isaac Newton",      "D",
    "Charles Darwin",    "A+", # so good at biology that we
    "Charles Darwin",    "A+" # listed him twice
)
inner_join(grades_maths2, grades_biology2, by = "name")
```

```
## # A tibble: 5 x 3
##   name           grade.x grade.y
##   <chr>          <chr>   <chr>
## 1 Marko Polo     D       F
## 2 Isaac Newton   A+      D
## 3 Isaac Newton   A+      D
## 4 Charles Darwin B       A+
## 5 Charles Darwin B       A+
```

inner_join(grades_maths2, grades_biology2, by = "grade")

```
## # A tibble: 5 x 3
##   name.x         grade name.y
##   <chr>          <chr> <chr>
## 1 Marko Polo     D     Isaac Newton
## 2 Isaac Newton   A+    Charles Darwin
## 3 Isaac Newton   A+    Charles Darwin
## 4 Isaac Newton   A+    Charles Darwin
## 5 Isaac Newton   A+    Charles Darwin
```

In the last join, you see that you can get the same line multiple times from an inner join. Combine the join with distinct() if you want to avoid this.

inner_join(grades_maths2, grades_biology2, by = "grade") %>%
    distinct()

```
## # A tibble: 2 x 3
##   name.x         grade name.y
##   <chr>          <chr> <chr>
## 1 Marko Polo     D     Isaac Newton
## 2 Isaac Newton   A+    Charles Darwin
```

The tables can have different variables—if they represent different relations—or they can share several or all variables. In the grades example, each table contains the same name/grade relationships, just for different classes. Therefore, they also share variables.

With shared variables, the data from the two tables can be differentiated by a suffix. The default (see previous example) is ".x" and ".y". You can change that using the suffix argument.

```
inner_join(
    grades_maths, grades_biology,
    by = "name", suffix = c(".maths", ".biology")
)

## # A tibble: 3 x 3
##    name            grade.maths grade.biology
##    <chr>           <chr>       <chr>
## 1 Marko Polo      D           F
## 2 Isaac Newton    A+          D
## 3 Charles Darwin  B           A+
```

Students might take different classes, and you have several choices on how to combine tables with different keys.

An inner_join() will only give you the rows where a key is in both tables.

```
grades_geography <- tribble(
    ~name,              ~grade,
    "Marko Polo",       "A",
    "Charles Darwin",   "A",
    "Immanuel Kant",    "A+"
)
grades_physics <- tribble(
    ~name,              ~grade,
    "Isaac Newton",     "A+",
```

```
    "Albert Einstein", "A+",
    "Charles Darwin",  "C"
)

inner_join(
    grades_geography, grades_physics,
    by = "name", suffix = c(".geography", ".physics")
)

## # A tibble: 1 x 3
##   name              grade.geography grade.physics
##   <chr>             <chr>           <chr>
## 1 Charles Darwin A                  C
```

The full_join() function, in contrast, gives you a table containing all keys. If a key is only found in one of the tables, the variables from the other table will be set to NA.

```
full_join(
    grades_geography, grades_physics,
    by = "name", suffix = c(".geography", ".physics")
)

## # A tibble: 5 x 3
##   name              grade.geography grade.physics
##   <chr>             <chr>           <chr>
## 1 Marko Polo        A               <NA>
## 2 Charles Darwin    A               C
## 3 Immanuel Kant     A+              <NA>
## 4 Isaac Newton      <NA>            A+
## 5 Albert Einstein <NA>              A+
```

If you want all keys from the left or right table (but not both left and right)—potentially with NA if the other table does not have the key—then you need left_join() or right_join().

left_join(
```
    grades_geography, grades_physics,
    by = "name", suffix = c(".geography", ".physics")
)
```

```
## # A tibble: 3 x 3
##    name              grade.geography grade.physics
##    <chr>             <chr>           <chr>
## 1 Marko Polo         A               <NA>
## 2 Charles Darwin     A               C
## 3 Immanuel Kant      A+              <NA>
```

right_join(
```
    grades_maths, grades_physics,
    by = "name", suffix = c(".maths", ".physics")
)
```

```
## # A tibble: 3 x 3
##    name              grade.maths grade.physics
##    <chr>             <chr>       <chr>
## 1 Isaac Newton       A+          A+
## 2 Albert Einstein    <NA>        A+
## 3 Charles Darwin     B           C
```

A semi_join() will give you all the rows in the first table that contains a key in the second table.

semi_join(
```
    grades_maths2, grades_biology2,
    by = "name", suffix = c(".geography", ".physics")
)
```

```
## # A tibble: 4 x 2
##    name             grade
##    <chr>            <chr>
## 1 Marko Polo        D
## 2 Isaac Newton      A+
## 3 Isaac Newton      A+
## 4 Charles Darwin    B
```

You only get one copy per row in the first table when a key matches, regardless of how many times the key appears in the second table.

This is unlike inner_join() where you get all combinations of rows from the two tables. The inner_join() is, therefore, not an analog to an inner_join() combined with a select().

inner_join(
    grades_maths2, grades_biology2,
    by = "name", suffix = **c**(".geography", ".physics")
) %>% **select**(1:2)

```
## # A tibble: 5 x 2
##    name             grade.geography
##    <chr>            <chr>
## 1 Marko Polo        D
## 2 Isaac Newton      A+
## 3 Isaac Newton      A+
## 4 Charles Darwin    B
## 5 Charles Darwin    B
```

You can still get multiple identical rows from a semi_join(). If the first table has duplicated rows, you will get the same duplications of the rows. If you do not want that, you can combine the join with distinct().

An anti_join() gives you all the rows in the first table where the key or keys are not found in the second table. Think of it as the complement of semi_join().

```
anti_join(
    grades_maths2, grades_physics,
    by = "name", suffix = c(".geography", ".physics")
)
```

```
## # A tibble: 1 x 2
##   name         grade
##   <chr>        <chr>
## 1 Marko Polo D
```

The join functions only take two tables as input, so you might wonder how you can combine multiple tables. One solution is to use purrr's reduce() function:

```
grades <- list(
    grades_maths, grades_biology,
    grades_geography, grades_physics
)
```

```
grades %>%
    reduce(full_join, by = "name") %>%
    rename_at(2:5, ~ c("maths", "biology", "geography", "physics
```

```
## # A tibble: 5 x 5
##   name              maths biology geography physics
##   <chr>             <chr> <chr>   <chr>     <chr>
## 1 Marko Polo        D     F       A         <NA>
## 2 Isaac Newton      A+    D       <NA>      A+
## 3 Charles Darwin    B     A+      A         C
## 4 Immanuel Kant     <NA>  <NA>    A+        <NA>
## 5 Albert Einstein   <NA>  <NA>    <NA>      A+
```

The `rename_at()` function works similarly to `select_at()`, and here, I use it to rename the last four columns.

Income in Fictional Countries

We had an example with income in fictional countries in Chapter 4. There, we did not have the proper tools needed to deal with missing data. We wanted to replace NA with the mean income for a country in rows with missing data, but the functions from `tidyr` didn't suffice. With `dplyr` we have the tools.

Recall the data:

```
mean_income <- tribble(
    ~country,   ~`2002`, ~`2003`, ~`2004`,  ~`2005`,
    "Numenor",  123456, 132654,     NA,   324156,
    "Westeros", 314256, NA,         NA,   465321,
    "Narnia",   432156, NA,         NA,       NA,
    "Gondor",   531426, 321465, 235461,   463521,
    "Laputa",    14235,  34125,  45123,    51234,
)
```

The following pipeline does what we want. I will explain it here, but you can try to work out the steps.

```
mean_income %>%
    gather(
        key = "year",
        value = "mean_income",
        -country
    ) %>% group_by(
        country
    ) %>% mutate(
        mean_per_country = mean(mean_income, na.rm = TRUE),
        mean_income = ifelse(
```

```
        is.na(mean_income),
        mean_per_country,
        mean_income
    )
  ) %>% spread(key = "year", value = "mean_income")
```

```
## # A tibble: 5 x 6
## # Groups:   country [5]
##   country mean_per_country `2002` `2003` `2004`
##   <chr>              <dbl>  <dbl>  <dbl>  <dbl>
## 1 Gondor           387968. 531426 3.21e5 2.35e5
## 2 Laputa            36179.  14235 3.41e4 4.51e4
## 3 Narnia           432156  432156 4.32e5 4.32e5
## 4 Numenor          193422  123456 1.33e5 1.93e5
## 5 Wester...        389788. 314256 3.90e5 3.90e5
## # ... with 1 more variable: `2005` <dbl>
```

The first step in the pipeline is reformatting the data. We saw how this work in Chapter 4.

```
mean_income %>%
    gather(
        key = "year",
        value = "mean_income",
        -country
    )
```

```
## # A tibble: 20 x 3
##    country year  mean_income
##    <chr>   <chr>       <dbl>
##  1 Numenor 2002       123456
##  2 Westeros 2002      314256
##  3 Narnia  2002       432156
##  4 Gondor  2002       531426
```

```
##  5 Laputa    2002      14235
##  6 Numenor   2003     132654
##  7 Westeros  2003        NA
##  8 Narnia    2003        NA
##  9 Gondor    2003     321465
## 10 Laputa    2003      34125
## 11 Numenor   2004        NA
## 12 Westeros  2004        NA
## 13 Narnia    2004        NA
## 14 Gondor    2004     235461
## 15 Laputa    2004      45123
## 16 Numenor   2005     324156
## 17 Westeros  2005     465321
## 18 Narnia    2005        NA
## 19 Gondor    2005     463521
## 20 Laputa    2005      51234
```

In the next two steps, we group by countries, so the means we calculate are per country and not the full data set, and then we compute the means and replace NA cells with them. To get a glimpse into the `mutate()` call, you can replace it with `summarise()` and see the mean of each country.

```
mean_income %>%
    gather(
        key = "year",
        value = "mean_income",
        -country
    ) %>% group_by(
        country
    ) %>% summarise(
        per_country_mean = mean(mean_income, na.rm = TRUE)
    )
```

```
## # A tibble: 5 x 2
##    country per_country_mean
##    <chr>              <dbl>
## 1 Gondor            387968.
## 2 Laputa             36179.
## 3 Narnia            432156
## 4 Numenor           193422
## 5 Westeros          389788.
```

In the next step, we can replace the missing data with their country mean in the mutate() call because we can refer to earlier columns when we create later columns in mutate().

If you had a pipeline where you had steps between the group_by() call and the mutate() call that sets the mean_income, you have to be careful. Do *not* put an ungroup() in there. The pipeline works because the mean_income is per country when we call mutate(). If we ungrouped, we would get the mean over *all* countries.

```
mean_income %>%
    gather(
        key = "year",
        value = "mean_income",
        -country
    ) %>% group_by(
        country
    ) %>% mutate(
        mean_per_country = mean(mean_income, na.rm = TRUE)
    )
```

```
## # A tibble: 20 x 4
## # Groups:    country [5]
##    country  year mean_income mean_per_country
##    <chr>    <chr>      <dbl>            <dbl>
##  1 Numenor  2002      123456           193422
##  2 Westeros 2002      314256          389788.
##  3 Narnia   2002      432156           432156
##  4 Gondor   2002      531426          387968.
##  5 Laputa   2002       14235           36179.
##  6 Numenor  2003      132654           193422
##  7 Westeros 2003          NA          389788.
##  8 Narnia   2003          NA           432156
##  9 Gondor   2003      321465          387968.
## 10 Laputa   2003       34125           36179.
## 11 Numenor  2004          NA           193422
## 12 Westeros 2004          NA          389788.
## 13 Narnia   2004          NA           432156
## 14 Gondor   2004      235461          387968.
## 15 Laputa   2004       45123           36179.
## 16 Numenor  2005      324156           193422
## 17 Westeros 2005      465321          389788.
## 18 Narnia   2005          NA           432156
## 19 Gondor   2005      463521          387968.
## 20 Laputa   2005       51234           36179.
```

In the last step, we ungroup and update the table before reformatting the tibble again.

```
mean_income %>%
    gather(
        key = "year",
        value = "mean_income",
        -country
```

```r
) %>% group_by(
    country
) %>% mutate(
    mean_per_country = mean(mean_income, na.rm = TRUE)
) %>% ungroup(
) %>% mutate(
    mean_income = ifelse(
        is.na(mean_income),
        mean_per_country,
        mean_income
    )
) %>% spread(key = "year", value = "mean_income")
```

```
## # A tibble: 5 x 6
##   country mean_per_country `2002` `2003` `2004`
##   <chr>              <dbl>  <dbl>  <dbl>  <dbl>
## 1 Gondor           387968. 531426 3.21e5 2.35e5
## 2 Laputa            36179.  14235 3.41e4 4.51e4
## 3 Narnia           432156  432156 4.32e5 4.32e5
## 4 Numenor          193422  123456 1.33e5 1.93e5
## 5 Wester...        389788. 314256 3.90e5 3.90e5
## # ...  with 1 more variable: `2005` <dbl>
```

This is how we replace all missing data with the mean for the corresponding countries.

CHAPTER 8

Working with Strings: stringr

The stringr package gives you functions for string manipulation. The package will be loaded when you load the tidyverse package:

```r
library(tidyverse)
```

You can also load the package alone using

```r
library(stringr)
```

Counting String Patterns

The str_count() function counts how many tokens a string contain, where tokens, for example, can be characters or words.

By default, str_count() will count the number of characters in a string.

```r
strings <- c(
    "Give me an ice cream",
    "Get yourself an ice cream",
    "We are all out of ice creams",
    "I scream, you scream, everybody loves ice cream.",
    "one ice cream,
```

© Thomas Mailund 2019
T. Mailund, *R Data Science Quick Reference*, https://doi.org/10.1007/978-1-4842-4894-2_8

```
    two ice creams,
    three ice creams",
    "I want an ice cream. Do you want an ice cream?"
)
str_count(strings)
```

[1] 20 25 28 48 55 46

For each of the strings in strings, we get the number of characters. The result is the same as we would get using nchar() (but not length() which would give us the length of the list containing them, six in this example).

You can be explicit in specifying that str_count() should count characters by giving it a boundary() option. This determines the boundary between tokens, that is, the units to count.

```
str_count(strings, boundary("character"))
```

[1] 20 25 28 48 55 46

If you want to count words instead, you can use boundary("word"):

```
str_count(strings, boundary("word"))
```

[1] 5 5 7 8 9 11

You can use two additional options to boundary(): "line_break" and "sentence." They use heuristics for determining how many line breaks and sentences the text contains dependent on a locale().

```
str_count(strings, boundary("line_break"))
```

[1] 5 5 7 8 11 11

```
str_count(strings, boundary("sentence"))
```

[1] 1 1 1 1 3 2

Notice that the line breaks are not the newlines in the text. The line breaks are where you would be expected to put newlines in your locale().

Finally, str_count() lets you count how often a substring is found in a string:

str_count(strings, "ice cream")

[1] 1 1 1 1 3 2

str_count(strings, "cream") # gets the screams as well

[1] 1 1 1 3 3 2

The pattern you ask str_count() to count is not just a string. It is a regular expression. Some characters take on special meaning in regular expressions.[1] For example, a dot represents any single character, not a full stop.

str_count(strings, ".")

[1] 20 25 28 48 53 46

If you want your pattern to be taken as a literal string and not a regular expression, you can wrap it in fixed():

str_count(strings, **fixed**("."))

[1] 0 0 0 1 0 1

Since the pattern is a regular expression, we can use it to count punctuation characters:

str_count(strings, "[:punct:]")

[1] 0 0 0 3 2 2

---

[1]Regular expressions are beyond the scope of this book, but if you are frequently working with strings, you might want to familiarize yourself with them.

Or the number of times ice cream(s) is at the end of the string:

str_count(strings, "ice creams?$")

[1] 1 1 1 0 1 0

The s? means zero or one s, and the $ means the end of the string or at the end of the string except that it might be followed by a punctuation mark.

str_count(strings, "ice creams?[:punct:]?$")

[1] 1 1 1 1 1 1

Splitting Strings

Sometimes you want to split a string based on some separator—not unlike how we split on commas in comma-separated value files. The stringr function for this is str_split().

We can, for example, split on a space:

```
strings <- c(
    "one",
    "two",
    "one two",
    "one two",
    "one. two."
)
str_split(strings, " ")
```

[[1]]
[1] "one"
##
[[2]]
[1] "two"

```
##
## [[3]]
## [1] "one" "two"
##
## [[4]]
## [1] "one" ""    ""    "two"
##
## [[5]]
## [1] "one." "two."
```

Since we are splitting on a single space, we get empty strings for "one   two" which contains three spaces.

You can use the boundary() function for splitting as well. For example, you can split a string into its words using boundary("word"):

str_split(strings, **boundary**("word"))

```
## [[1]]
## [1] "one"
##
## [[2]]
## [1] "two"
##
## [[3]]
## [1] "one" "two"
##
## [[4]]
## [1] "one" "two"
##
## [[5]]
## [1] "one" "two"
```

When we do this, we get rid of the empty strings from the previous example, and we also get rid of the full stops in the last string.

Capitalizing Strings

You can use the str_to_lower() to transform a string into all lowercase.

```
macdonald <- "Old MACDONALD had a farm."
str_to_lower(macdonald)
```

[1] "old macdonald had a farm."

Similarly, you can use str_to_upper() to translate it into all uppercase.

```
str_to_upper(macdonald)
```

[1] "OLD MACDONALD HAD A FARM."

If you use str_to_sentence(), the first character is uppercase and the rest lowercase.

```
str_to_sentence(macdonald)
```

[1] "Old macdonald had a farm."

The str_to_title() function will capitalize all words in your string.

```
str_to_title(macdonald)
```

[1] "Old Macdonald Had A Farm."

Wrapping, Padding, and Trimming

If you want to wrap strings, that is, add newlines, so they fit into a certain width, you can use str_wrap().

```
strings <- c(
    "Give me an ice cream",
    "Get yourself an ice cream",
    "We are all out of ice creams",
    "I scream, you scream, everybody loves ice cream.",
    "one ice cream,
    two ice creams,
    three ice creams",
    "I want an ice cream. Do you want an ice cream?"
)
str_wrap(strings)
```

```
## [1] "Give me an ice cream"
## [2] "Get yourself an ice cream"
## [3] "We are all out of ice creams"
## [4] "I scream, you scream, everybody loves ice cream."
## [5] "one ice cream, two ice creams, three ice creams"
## [6] "I want an ice cream. Do you want an ice cream?"
```

The default width is 80 characters, but you can change that using the width argument.

```
str_wrap(strings, width = 10)
```

```
## [1] "Give me an\nice cream"
## [2] "Get\nyourself\nan ice\ncream"
## [3] "We are all\nout of ice\ncreams"
## [4] "I scream,\nyou\nscream,\neverybody\nloves ice\ncream."
## [5] "one ice\ncream,\ntwo ice\ncreams,\nthree ice\ncreams"
## [6] "I want an\nice cream.\nDo you\nwant an\nice cream?"
```

You can indent the first line in the strings while wrapping them using the indent argument.

str_wrap(strings, width = 10, indent = 2)

```
## [1] " Give me an\nice cream"
## [2] " Get\nyourself\nan ice\ncream"
## [3] " We are all\nout of ice\ncreams"
## [4] " I scream,\nyou\nscream,\neverybody\nloves ice\ncream."
## [5] " one ice\ncream,\ntwo ice\ncreams,\nthree ice\ncreams"
## [6] " I want an\nice cream.\nDo you\nwant an\nice cream?"
```

If you want your string to be left, right, or center justified, you can use str_pad().

The default is right-justifying strings.

str_pad(strings, width = 50)

```
## [1] "                         Give me an ice cream"
## [2] "                     Get yourself an ice cream"
## [3] "                    We are all out of ice creams"
## [4] " I scream, you scream, everybody loves ice cream."
## [5] "one ice cream,\n two ice creams,\n three ice creams"
## [6] " I want an ice cream. Do you want an ice cream?"
```

If you want to left justify instead, you can pass "right" to the side argument.

str_pad(strings, width = 50, side = "right")

```
## [1] "Give me an ice cream"
## [2] "Get yourself an ice cream"
## [3] "We are all out of ice creams"
## [4] "I scream, you scream, everybody loves ice cream."
## [5] "one ice cream,\n two ice creams,\n three ice creams"
## [6] "I want an ice cream. Do you want an ice cream?"
```

You need to use "right" to left justify because the side argument determines which side to pad, and for left-justified text, the padding is on the right.

If you want to center your text, you should use "both"; you are padding both on the left and on the right.

```
str_pad(strings, width = 50, side = "both")
```

```
## [1] "              Give me an ice cream              "
## [2] "            Get yourself an ice cream           "
## [3] "            We are all out of ice creams        "
## [4] " I scream, you scream, everybody loves ice cream."
## [5] "one ice cream,\n two ice creams,\n three ice creams"
## [6] " I want an ice cream. Do you want an ice cream?"
```

In these padding examples, we do not keep the lengths of the strings below the padding width. If a string is longer than the padding width, it is unchanged. You can use the str_trunc() function to cut the width down to a certain value. For example, we could truncate all the strings to width 25 before we pad them:

```
strings %>% str_trunc(25) %>% str_pad(width = 25, side = "left")
```

```
## [1] "     Give me an ice cream"
## [2] "Get yourself an ice cream"
## [3] "We are all out of ice ..."
## [4] "I scream, you scream, ..."
## [5] " one ice cream,\n two..."
## [6] "I want an ice cream. D..."
```

The str_trim() function removes whitespace to the left and right of a string:

```
str_trim(c(
    " one small coke",
    "two large cokes ",
    " three medium cokes "
))
```

```
## [1] "one small coke" "two large cokes"
## [3] "three medium cokes"
```

It keeps whitespace inside the string.

Since str_trim() does not touch whitespace that is not flanking on the left or right, we cannot use it to remove extra spaces inside our string. For example, if we have two spaces between two words, as in the following example, str_trim() leaves them alone.

```
str_trim(c(
    " one small coke",
    "two large cokes ",
    " three medium cokes "
))
```

```
## [1] "one small coke" "two large cokes"
## [3] "three medium cokes"
```

If we want the two spaces to be shortened into a single space, we can use str_squish() instead.

```
str_squish(c(
    " one small coke",
    "two large cokes ",
    " three medium cokes "
))
```

```
## [1] "one small coke" "two large cokes"
## [3] "three medium cokes"
```

Detecting Substrings

To check if a substring is found in another string, you can use str_
detect().

str_detect(strings, "me")

```
## [1] TRUE FALSE FALSE FALSE FALSE FALSE
```

str_detect(strings, "I")

```
## [1] FALSE FALSE FALSE TRUE FALSE TRUE
```

str_detect(strings, "cream")

```
## [1] TRUE TRUE TRUE TRUE TRUE TRUE
```

The pattern is a regular expression, so to test for ice cream followed by a full stop, you cannot search for "ice cream.".

str_detect(strings, "ice cream.")

```
## [1] FALSE FALSE TRUE TRUE TRUE TRUE
```

You can, again, use a fixed() string.

str_detect(strings, **fixed**("ice cream."))

```
## [1] FALSE FALSE FALSE TRUE FALSE TRUE
```

Alternatively, you can escape the dot.

str_detect(strings, "ice cream\\.")

```
## [1] FALSE FALSE FALSE TRUE FALSE TRUE
```

You can test if a substring is *not* found in a string by setting the negate argument to TRUE.

str_detect(strings, **fixed**("ice cream."), negate = TRUE)

[1] TRUE TRUE TRUE FALSE TRUE FALSE

Two special case functions test for a string at the start or end of a string:

str_starts(strings, "I")

[1] FALSE FALSE FALSE TRUE FALSE TRUE

str_ends(strings, **fixed**("."))

[1] FALSE FALSE FALSE TRUE FALSE FALSE

If you want to know where a substring is found, you can use str_locate(). It will give you the start and the end index where it found a match.

str_locate(strings, "ice cream")

```
##        start end
## [1,]     12  20
## [2,]     17  25
## [3,]     19  27
## [4,]     39  47
## [5,]      5  13
## [6,]     11  19
```

Here you get a start and an end index for each string, but string number six has more than one occurrence of the pattern.

strings[6]

[1] "I want an ice cream. Do you want an ice cream?"

You only get the indices for the first occurrence when you use str_locate().

str_locate(strings[6], "ice cream")

```
##      start end
## [1,]   11   19
```

The function str_locate_all() gives you all occurrences.

str_locate_all(strings[6], "ice cream")

```
## [[1]]
##      start end
## [1,]   11   19
## [2,]   37   45
```

If you want the start and end points of the strings *between* the occurrences, you can use invert_match().

```
ice_cream_locations <- str_locate_all(strings[6], "ice cream")
ice_cream_locations
```

```
## [[1]]
##      start end
## [1,]   11   19
## [2,]   37   45
```

invert_match(ice_cream_locations[[1]])

```
##      start end
## [1,]     0  10
## [2,]    20  36
## [3,]    46  -1
```

Extracting Substrings

To extract a substring matching a pattern, you can use str_extract(). It gives you the first substring that matches a regular expression.

```
str_extract(strings, "(s|ice )cream\\w*")
```

```
## [1] "ice cream" "ice cream" "ice creams"
## [4] "scream"    "ice cream" "ice cream"
```

It only gives you the first match, but if you want all substrings that match you can use str_extract_all().

```
strings[4]
```

```
## [1] "I scream, you scream, everybody loves ice cream."
```

```
str_extract(strings[4], "(s|ice )cream\\w*")
```

```
## [1] "scream"
```

```
str_extract_all(strings[4], "(s|ice )cream\\w*")
```

```
## [[1]]
## [1] "scream"    "scream"    "ice cream"
```

Transforming Strings

We can replace a substring that matches a pattern with some other string.

```
lego_str <- str_replace(strings, "ice cream[s]?", "LEGO")
lego_str
```

```
## [1] "Give me an LEGO"
## [2] "Get yourself an LEGO"
## [3] "We are all out of LEGO"
## [4] "I scream, you scream, everybody loves LEGO."
```

```
## [5] "one LEGO,\n two ice creams,\n three ice creams"
## [6] "I want an LEGO. Do you want an ice cream?"

lego_str <- str_replace(lego_str, "an LEGO", "a LEGO")
lego_str

## [1] "Give me a LEGO"
## [2] "Get yourself a LEGO"
## [3] "We are all out of LEGO"
## [4] "I scream, you scream, everybody loves LEGO."
## [5] "one LEGO,\n two ice creams,\n three ice creams"
## [6] "I want a LEGO. Do you want an ice cream?"
```

These two replacement operators can be written as a pipeline to make the code more Tidyverse-y:

```
strings %>%
    str_replace("ice cream[s]?", "LEGO") %>%
    str_replace("an LEGO", "a LEGO")

## [1] "Give me a LEGO"
## [2] "Get yourself a LEGO"
## [3] "We are all out of LEGO"
## [4] "I scream, you scream, everybody loves LEGO."
## [5] "one LEGO,\n two ice creams,\n three ice creams"
## [6] "I want a LEGO. Do you want an ice cream?"
```

Like most of the previous functions, the function only affects the first match. To replace all occurrences, you need str_replace_all().

```
strings %>%
    str_replace_all("ice cream[s]?", "LEGO") %>%
    str_replace_all("an LEGO", "a LEGO")
```

```
## [1] "Give me a LEGO"
## [2] "Get yourself a LEGO"
## [3] "We are all out of LEGO"
## [4] "I scream, you scream, everybody loves LEGO."
## [5] "one LEGO,\n two LEGO,\n three LEGO"
## [6] "I want a LEGO. Do you want a LEGO?"
```

You can refer back to matching groups in the replacement string, something you will be familiar with for regular expressions.

```
us_dates <- c(
    valentines = "2/14",
    my_birthday = "2/15",
    # no one knows but let's just go
    # with this
    jesus_birthday = "12/24"
)
# US date format to a more sane format
str_replace(us_dates, "(.*)/(.*)", "\\2/\\1")
```

```
## [1] "14/2" "15/2" "24/12"
```

The str_dup() function duplicates a string, that is, it repeats a string several times.

```
str_c(
    "NA",
    str_dup("-NA", times = 7),
    " BATMAN!"
)
```

```
## [1] "NA-NA-NA-NA-NA-NA-NA-NA BATMAN!"
```

Here we also used `str_c()` to concatenate strings. This function works differently from `c()`; the latter will create a vector of multiple strings, while the former will create one string.

```
# -- concatenation ----------------------------------------
c("foo", "bar", "baz")

## [1] "foo" "bar" "baz"

str_c("foo", "bar", "baz")

## [1] "foobarbaz"
```

A more direct way to extract and modify a substring is using `str_sub()`. It lets you extract a substring specified by a start and an end index, and if you assign to it, you replace the substring. The `str_sub()` function is less powerful than the other functions as it doesn't work on regular expressions, but because of this, it is also easier to understand.

If you do not know where a substring is found, you must first find it. You can use `str_locate()` for this.

```
my_string <- "this is my string"
my_location <- str_locate(my_string, "my")
my_location

##      start end
## [1,]     9  10

s <- my_location[,"start"]
e <- my_location[,"end"]
str_sub(my_string, s, e)

## [1] "my"


my_string_location <- str_locate(my_string, "string")
s <- my_string_location[,"start"]
```

```
e <- my_string_location[,"end"]
str_sub(my_string, s, e)
```

```
## [1] "string"
```

```
your_string <- my_string
s <- my_location[,"start"]
e <- my_location[,"end"]
str_sub(your_string, s, e) <- "your"
your_string
```

```
## [1] "this is your string"
```

```
your_banana <- your_string
your_string_location <- str_locate(your_string, "string")
s <- your_string_location[,"start"]
e <- your_string_location[,"end"]
str_sub(your_banana, s, e) <- "banana"
your_banana
```

```
## [1] "this is your banana"
```

When you assign to a call to str_sub(), it looks like you are modifying a string. This is an illusion. Assignment functions create new data and change the data that a variable refers to. So, if you have more than one reference to a string, be careful. Only one variable will point to the new value; the remaining will point to the old string. This is not specific to str_sub() but for R in general, and it is a potential source of errors.

```
my_string
```

```
## [1] "this is my string"
```

```
your_string
```

```
## [1] "this is your string"
```

```
your_banana
```

```
## [1] "this is your banana"
```

If you often write code to produce standard reports, virtually the same text each time but with a few selected values changed, then you are going to love str_glue(). This does precisely what you want. You give str_glue() a template string, a string with the mutable pieces in curly brackets. The result of calling str_glue() is the template text but with the values in the curly brackets replaced by what R expression they contain.

The most straightforward use is when the template refers to variables.

```
macdonald <- "Old MacDonald"
eieio <- "E-I-E-I-O"
str_glue("{macdonald} had a farm. {eieio}")
```

```
## Old MacDonald had a farm. E-I-E-I-O
```

The variables do not need to be global. They can also be named arguments to str_glue().

```
str_glue(
    "{macdonald} had a farm. {eieio}",
    macdonald = "Thomas",
    eieio = "He certainly did not!"
)
```

```
## Thomas had a farm. He certainly did not!
```

Generally, you can put R expressions in the curly brackets, and the result of evaluating the expressions will be what is inserted into the template string.

```
str_glue(
    "{str_dup(\"NA-\", times = 7)}NA BATMAN!"
)
```

```
## NA-NA-NA-NA-NA-NA-NA-NA  BATMAN!
```

```
x <- seq(1:10)
str_glue(
  "Holy {mean(x)} BATMAN!"
  )
```

```
## Holy 5.5 BATMAN!
```

CHAPTER 9

Working with Factors: forcats

If you work with categorical data, you can often represent the categories by strings. Strings have some drawbacks, however. For example, a spelling mistake can easily go undiscovered. If you want your categories ordered, then the lexicographical order on strings will not always be the order you need. As an alternative to strings for categories is factors. In this chapter, we look at the functionality that the forcats package provides for creating and manipulating factors.

The package is loaded when you import tidyverse,

```
library(tidyverse)
```

but you can also load it explicitly

```
library(forcats)
```

Creating Factors

The built-in factor() function is still an excellent choice to build a factor from scratch, especially if you want to specify the levels of the factor when you create it.

© Thomas Mailund 2019
T. Mailund, *R Data Science Quick Reference*, https://doi.org/10.1007/978-1-4842-4894-2_9

If you create a factor without explicitly specifying the levels, you get a level per unique element in the input.

```
factor(c("A", "C", "B"))
```

```
## [1] A C B
## Levels: A B C
```

Otherwise, you get the levels you pass to the `levels` argument.

```
factor(c("A", "C", "B"), levels = c("A", "B", "C", "D"))
```

```
## [1] A C B
## Levels: A B C D
```

```
factor(c("A", "C", "B"), levels = c("D", "C", "B", "A"))
```

```
## [1] A C B
## Levels: D C B A
```

If you have a value that is not found in the levels, it will be set to NA.

```
factor(c("A", "C", "B"), levels = c("A", "B"))
```

```
## [1] A<NA> B
## Levels: A B
```

The `factor()` function is usually the right choice for creating factors. The function is not generic, however, so if you want a way to translate a data structure you have implemented yourself, one that needs a specific method to do so, then you might want to specialize `as_factor()` from `forcats`.

If you specialize `as_factor()`, you can do anything you want, but on normal vectors, `as_factor()` works similarly to `as.factor()` from base R. The two functions differ, though, in how they set levels. If you use `as.factor()`, the levels will be sorted.

```
f1 <- as.factor(c("C", "B", "B", "A", "D"))
f1 # levels ordered alphabetically
```

```
## [1] C B B A D
## Levels: A B C D
```

With as_factor(), the levels are in the order they appear in the input.

```
f2 <- as_factor(c("C", "B", "B", "A", "D"))
f2 # levels in the order they appear in the input
```

```
## [1] C B B A D
## Levels: C B A D
```

Concatenation

If you have two factors, then you can concatenate them using fct_c(). The levels of the resulting factor are the union of the levels of the input factors. The order of the levels depends on the order of the input factors. The levels in the first factor go first, then the levels in the second. If the factors share levels, then the order is determined by the first vector.

For example, consider again the factors f1 and f2 from the preceding example.

```
f1
```

```
## [1] C B B A D
## Levels: A B C D
```

```
f2
```

```
## [1] C B B A D
## Levels: C B A D
```

They have the same levels, but they have them in different orders. If we concatenate f1 with f2, we get the levels in the order from f1.

fct_c(f1, f2)

```
## [1] C B B A D C B B A D
## Levels: A B C D
```

If we concatenate f2 with f1, then the levels are ordered as in f2.

fct_c(f2, f1)

```
## [1] C B B A D C B B A D
## Levels: C B A D
```

Consider now a factor that has levels not found in f1, for example, this:

f3 <- **as_factor**(**c**("X", "Y", "A"))

It shares one level, A, with f1, but X and Y are unique to f3. If we concatenate, with f1 as the first argument, the new levels are included but after the factors from f1 (and the shared factor A).

fct_c(f1, f3)

```
## [1] C B B A D X Y A
## Levels: A B C D X Y
```

If we concatenate with f3 as the first argument, then f3's levels come first.

fct_c(f3, f1)

```
## [1] X Y A C B B A D
## Levels: X Y A B C D
```

You can concatenate more than one factor using fct_c(). The rules
are the same as for two factors.

fct_c(f1, f2, f3)

```
## [1] C B B A D C B B A D X Y A
## Levels: A B C D X Y
```

fct_c(f2, f3, f1)

```
## [1] C B B A D X Y A C B B A D
## Levels: C B A D X Y
```

fct_c(f3, f1, f2)

```
## [1] X Y A C B B A D C B B A D
## Levels: X Y A B C D
```

If you have several factors that do not have the same levels, but you
want them to have (without concatenating them), you can use fct_
unify(). It takes a list of factors and gives you a list of factors where they all
have as levels the union of the levels of the input.

fct_unify(fs = **list**(f1, f2, f3))

```
## [[1]]
## [1] C B B A D
## Levels: A B C D X Y
##
## [[2]]
## [1] C B B A D
## Levels: A B C D X Y
##
## [[3]]
## [1] X Y A
## Levels: A B C D X Y
```

Projection

It happens that your categorical data is too fine-grained and you want
to group categories into larger classes. If so, the function you want is
fct_collapse(). It lets you map your existing levels to new levels. Its
first argument is a factor and after that you provide named arguments.
As parameters to the named arguments, you must provide a list of level
names. Each name becomes a level, and that level will contain the
elements in the list you give as the argument.

```
fct_collapse(
    fct_c(f3, f1),
    a = c("A", "X"),
    b = c("B", "Y"),
    c = c("C", "D")
)
```

```
## [1] a b a c b b a c
## Levels: a b c
```

You do not need to remap all levels. Those you do not map will stay as
they were.

```
fct_collapse(
    fct_c(f3, f1),
    a = c("A", "X"),
    b = c("B", "Y")
)
```

```
## [1] a b a C b b a D
## Levels: a b C D
```

If you only want to rename and not collapse levels, you can use fct_
recode().

186

```
f1
```

```
## [1] C B B A D
## Levels: A B C D
```

```
fct_recode(f1, a = "A", b = "B")
```

```
## [1] C b b a D
## Levels: a b C D
```

```
fct_recode(f1, X = "A", X = "B", Y = "C", Y = "D")
```

```
## [1] Y X X X Y
## Levels: X Y
```

If you want to reduce the number of levels based on how many elements they have, rather than merge the levels in an explicitly specified way, then you can use fct_lump(). You can merge levels such that you keep the n levels with the most elements, for example, for $n = 5$ and $n = 2$:

```
f <- factor(sample(1:10, 20, replace = TRUE), levels = 1:10)
table(f)
```

```
## f
## 1 2 3 4 5 6 7 8 9 10
## 0 2 5 2 1 3 1 1 3  2
```

```
f %>% fct_lump(n = 5, other_level = "X") %>% table()
```

```
## .
## 2 3 4 6 9 10 X
## 2 5 2 3 3  2 3
```

```
f %>% fct_lump(n = 2, other_level = "X") %>% table()
```

```
## .
## 3 6 9 X
## 5 3 3 9
```

You see more than five and two levels here, even though we called
fct_lump() with *n* = 5 and *n* = 2. If there are several levels with the same
number of elements, the function doesn't pick random ones to keep. You
get all with the largest counts.

If you use a negative number, you get the least common categories.

```
f %>% fct_lump(n = -2, other_level = "X") %>% table()

## .
## 1 5 7 8  X
## 0 1 1 1 17
```

Instead of picking the number of categories you want, you can require
that they contain at least or at most a fraction of the data. For that, you use
the prop parameter. To get the levels that contain at least 10% of the data,
you use prop = 0.1:

```
f %>% fct_lump(prop = 0.1, other_level = "X") %>% table()

## .
## 3 6 9 X
## 5 3 3 9
```

If you want the categories that contain less than 10% of the data,
you use prop as well but with a negative value. To get the categories that
contain at most 10%, you use

```
f %>% fct_lump(prop = -0.1, other_level = "X") %>% table()

## .
## 1 2 4 5 7 8 10  X
## 0 2 2 1 1 1  2 11
```

A more straightforward way to map categories is to map a fixed
number to a new category. The fct_other() lets you pick a list of
categories to keep or drop. If you keep categories, then all the others are

put in the same "other" category. If you drop categories, then those you drop are placed in an "other" category. You can name the "other" category using the argument other_level.

```
f %>% fct_other(keep = 1:5, other_level = "X")
```

```
## [1] 3 X X 3 2 X X X X 2 3 5 4 X 3 3 4 X X X
## Levels: 1 2 3 4 5 X
```

```
f %>% fct_other(drop = 1:5, other_level = "X")
```

```
## [1] X 7 10 X X 8 6 9 10 X X X X 6 X
## [16] X X 9 6 9
## Levels: 6 7 8 9 10 X
```

Sometimes what you want is even simpler. You have levels that are not found in the actual data. You can get rid of the empty levels using fct_drop( )

```
f1
```

```
## [1] C B B A D
## Levels: A B C D
```

```
levels(f1) <- LETTERS[1:10]
f1
```

```
## [1] C B B A D
## Levels: A B C D E F G H I J
```

```
fct_drop(f1)
```

```
## [1] C B B A D
## Levels: A B C D
```

Adding Levels

The opposite of fct_drop() is adding extra levels. Assigning to levels(), as we did previously, will add levels that are not necessarily in the factor, but it might also rename the levels at the same time. The levels are renamed; you are not just adding to them. This happened to f1. Its original levels, 1, 2, 3, and 4, were replaced with A, B, C, and D when we added the new levels.

With the fct_expand() function, you can add levels that are not in your factor, and any levels that are already in the data will be ignored.

f1

```
## [1] C B B A D
## Levels: A B C D E F G H I J
```

f3

```
## [1] X Y A
## Levels: X Y A
```

fct_expand(f1, **levels**(f3))

```
## [1] C B B A D
## Levels: A B C D E F G H I J X Y
```

Missing data is not considered missing data by R, and often we can simply ignore it. Sometimes, however, there is information in missing data that we need to consider. Since R doesn't play well with missing data in many statistical tests, it is best to translate it into a category that R *will* work with. You can use fct_explicit_na() to map all missing data into a new category:

f2

```
## [1] C B B A D
## Levels: C B A D
```

```
fna <- f2
fna[2] <- NA
fna[3] <- NA
fna
```

```
## [1] C <NA> <NA> A D
## Levels: C B A D
```

```
fna <- fct_explicit_na(fna, na_level = "Missing")
fna
```

```
## [1] C Missing Missing A D
## Levels: C B A D Missing
```

Reorder Levels

If you construct a factor with factor(), you can control the order of the levels using the levels argument. If you use as.factor(), your levels will get sorted, and if you use as_factor(), they will be sorted in the order that the levels appear in the data. You can map between these orders if you want to, though.

If you have a factor created with factor() without specifying the levels, then the levels will be all elements seen in the input sorted in their natural order.

```
f <- factor(sample(LETTERS[1:5], 10, replace = TRUE))
f
```

```
##  [1] E D B B A C C E A E
## Levels: A B C D E
```

The function fct_inorder() will order your levels to match the order that the categories are seen in the data—the order you get from as_factor().

fct_inorder(f)

```
## [1] E D B B A C C E A E
## Levels: E D B A C
```

The functions for reordering levels can also make the factors ordered.[1]

fct_inorder(f, ordered = TRUE)

```
## [1] E D B B A C C E A E
## Levels: E < D < B < A < C
```

If you want to sort the levels, you do not need forcats functions. The plain old factor() will do nicely.

factor(f, levels = **sort**(**levels**(f)))

```
## [1] E D B B A C C E A E
## Levels: A B C D E
```

factor(f, levels = **sort**(**levels**(f)), ordered = TRUE)

```
## [1] E D B B A C C E A E
## Levels: A < B < C < D < E
```

---

[1]Ordered factors are not just factors with the levels sorted. Ordered factors specify that there is an order on the levels. Regardless of how the levels are sorted in a factor that is not ordered, the categories do not have a natural order to them. This is used in some statistical tests.

You can order levels by their frequency in the factor using `fct_infreq()`

table(f)

```
## f
## A B C D E
## 2 2 2 1 3
```

fct_infreq(f)

```
##  [1] E D B B A C C E A E
## Levels: E A B C D
```

f %>% **fct_infreq**() %>% **table**()

```
## .
## E A B C D
## 3 2 2 2 1
```

f %>% **fct_infreq**(ordered = TRUE)

```
##  [1] E D B B A C C E A E
## Levels: E < A < B < C < D
```

f %>% **fct_infreq**() %>% **fct_rev**() %>% **table**()

```
## .
## D C B A E
## 1 2 2 2 3
```

In the last example, I reversed the levels, so the order is smallest to largest rather than largest to smallest. The function `fct_rev()` reverses the levels; a frequent use for this is when you plot with an axis given by the factor. There, the order is given by the levels, and you might want it reversed.

Working with Dates: lubridate

The lubridate package is essential for working with dates and fits well with the Tidyverse. It is not, however, loaded when you import the tidyverse package, so you need to explicitly load it.

library(lubridate)

Time Points

You can create dates and dates with time-of-day information using variations of the ymd() function. The letters y, m, and d stand for year, month, and day, respectively. With ymd() you should write your data in a format that puts the year first, the month second, and the day last. The function is very flexible in what it can parse as a date.

ymd("1975 Feb 15")

[1] "1975-02-15"

ymd("19750215")

[1] "1975-02-15"

© Thomas Mailund 2019
T. Mailund, *R Data Science Quick Reference*, https://doi.org/10.1007/978-1-4842-4894-2_10

ymd("1975/2/15")

[1] "1975-02-15"

ymd("1975-02-15")

[1] "1975-02-15"

You can permute the y, m, and d letters if the order of year, month, and day is different. Each permutation gives you a parser that will interpret its input in the specified order.

dmy("150275")

[1] "1975-02-15"

mdy("February 15th 1975")

[1] "1975-02-15"

If you want to add a time of the day to your date, you can add an hour, an hour and a minute, or an hour, a minute, and a second by using _h(), _hm() and _hms() variants of the ymd() functions.

dmy_h("15/2/1975 2pm")

[1] "1975-02-15 14:00:00 UTC"

dmy_hm("15/2/1975 14:30")

[1] "1975-02-15 14:30:00 UTC"

dmy_hms("15/2/1975 14:30:10")

[1] "1975-02-15 14:30:10 UTC"

If you have a time object

x <- **dmy_hms**("15/2/1975 14:30:10")

then you can extract its components through dedicated functions:

```
c(day(x), month(x), year(x))
```

```
## [1]   15   2 1975
```

```
c(hour(x), minute(x), second(x))
```

```
## [1] 14 30 10
```

```
c(week(x), # The week in the year
  wday(x), # The day in the week
  yday(x)) # The day in the year
```

```
## [1] 7 7 46
```

These functions have corresponding assignment functions that you can use to modify the components of the time point.

```
minute(x) <- 15
wday(x) <- 42
x
```

```
## [1] "1975-03-22 14:15:10 UTC"
```

Time Zones

When you add a time of day, a time zone is also necessary. After all, we do not know what time a given hour is before we know which time zone we are in. If I tell you that I am going to call you at two o'clock, you can't assume that it is two o'clock in your time zone.[1] Unless you tell the functions otherwise, they will assume UTC is the time zone. You can specify another time zone via the tz argument.

---

[1] I am in CEST right now. In Denmark, we switch between CEST and CET depending on daylight saving time.

```
x <- dmy_hm(
  "15/2/1975 14:00",
  tz = "Europe/Copenhagen"
)
x
```

```
## [1] "1975-02-15 14:00:00 CET"
```

You can take a time point in one time zone and move it to another in two different ways. You set the time zone and pretend that the day and time of day were already in this time zone. That is, you can just change the time zone attribute of the object and not touch the time information. You can do this using the function force_tz().

```
force_tz().
```

```
force_tz(
  dmy_hm("15/2/1975 14:00",
         tz = "Europe/Copenhagen"),
  tz = "Europe/London"
)
```

```
## [1] "1975-02-15 14:00:00 GMT"
```

A much more likely situation is that you want to know at what a time point in one time zone was in another time zone. For example, if I promise to call you at two o'clock in Denmark, and you are in the UK, you can translate the time from my time zone to yours using with_tz().

```
with_tz(x, tz = "Europe/London")
```

```
## [1] "1975-02-15 13:00:00 GMT"
```

Time Intervals

If you have two time points, you also have a time interval: the time between the two points. You can create an interval object from two time points using the interval() function.

```
start <- dmy("02 11 1949")
end <- dmy("15 02 1975")
interval(start, end)
```

```
## [1] 1949-11-02 UTC--1975-02-15 UTC
```

The infix operator %--% does the same thing.

```
start %--% end
```

```
## [1] 1949-11-02 UTC--1975-02-15 UTC
```

You can get the start and end points of an interval using int_start() and int_end().

```
int <- interval(start, end)
int
```

```
## [1] 1949-11-02 UTC--1975-02-15 UTC
```

```
int_start(int)
```

```
## [1] "1949-11-02 UTC"
```

```
int_end(int)
```

```
## [1] "1975-02-15 UTC"
```

The start point does not have to be before the endpoint. You can define an interval that starts after it ends.

```
end %--% start
```

```
## [1] 1975-02-15 UTC--1949-11-02 UTC
```

int_start(start %--% end)

```
## [1] "1949-11-02 UTC"
```

int_start(end %--% start)

```
## [1] "1975-02-15 UTC"
```

You can flip an interval using int_flip().

int_flip(end %--% start)

```
## [1] 1949-11-02 UTC--1975-02-15 UTC
```

The function int_standardize() will flip the interval if the start point comes after the endpoint but otherwise will leave the interval as it is.

int_standardize(start %--% end)

```
## [1] 1949-11-02 UTC--1975-02-15 UTC
```

int_standardize(end %--% start)

```
## [1] 1949-11-02 UTC--1975-02-15 UTC
```

The int_length() will give you the length of an interval in seconds.

```
x <- now()
int <- interval(x, x + minutes(1))
int
```

```
## [1] 2019-06-18 09:28:32 CEST--2019-06-18 09:29:32 CEST
```

int_length(int)

```
## [1] 60
```

```
int <- interval(x, x + minutes(20))
int
```

```
## [1] 2019-06-18 09:28:32 CEST--2019-06-18 09:48:32 CEST
```

int_length(int) / 60

```
## [1] 20
```

You can check if a point is in an interval using the %within% operator.

ymd("1867 05 02") %within% int

```
## [1] FALSE
```

ymd("1959 04 23") %within% int

```
## [1] FALSE
```

You can update the start and end point in an interval by assigning to int_start() or int_end():

```
int_start(int) <- dmy("19 Aug 1950")
int
```

```
## [1] 1950-08-19 01:00:00 CET--2019-06-18 09:48:32 CEST
```

```
int_end(int) <- dmy("19 Sep 1950")
int
```

```
## [1] 1950-08-19 01:00:00 CET--1950-09-19 01:00:00 CET
```

You can move the entire interval by a fixed amount. For example, you can move the interval one month forward using

```
int_shift(int, months(1))
```

```
## [1] 1950-09-19 01:00:00 CET--1950-10-19 01:00:00 CET
```

Given two intervals, the int_overlaps() function checks if they overlap.

```
int1 <- interval(dmy("19 oct 1950"), dmy("25 nov 1951"))
int2 <- interval(dmy("19 oct 1948"), dmy("25 aug 1951"))
int3 <- interval(dmy("19 oct 1981"), dmy("25 aug 2051"))
c(int, int1)
```

```
## [1] 1950-08-19 01:00:00 CET--1950-09-19 01:00:00 CET
## [2] 1950-10-19 01:00:00 CET--1951-11-25 01:00:00 CET
```

```
# int1 is contained in int
int_overlaps(int, int1)
```

```
## [1] FALSE
```

```
# int2 starts before int but they overlap
int_overlaps(int, int2)
```

```
## [1] TRUE
```

```
# no overlap
int_overlaps(int, int3)
```

```
## [1] FALSE
```

The function int_aligns() checks if any of the four start/end points are equal. That is, either the start or the end point of the first interval must be equal to at least one of the points in the second interval.

The preceding four intervals we have created do not have shared interval endpoints.

```
c(
  int_aligns(int, int1),
  int_aligns(int, int2),
  int_aligns(int, int3)
)
```

[1] FALSE FALSE FALSE

Test it with intervals that share end points and test int_aligns():

```
int4 <- interval(int_start(int), int_end(int) + years(3))
int5 <- int_shift(int4, -years(3))
int6 <- int_shift(int5, -years(3))
```

```
c(
  int_aligns(int, int4), # share start
  int_aligns(int, int5), # share end
  int_aligns(int, int6) # overlaps but does not share endpoints
)
```

[1] TRUE TRUE FALSE

CHAPTER 11

Working with Models: broom and modelr

There are many models to which you can fit your data, from classical statistical models to modern machine learning methods, and a thorough exploration of R packages that support this is well beyond the scope of this book. The main concern when choosing and fitting models is not the syntax, and this book is, after all, a syntax reference. We will look at two packages that aim at making a tidy interface to models.

The two packages, broom and modelr, are not loaded with tidyverse so you must load them individually.

```
library(broom)
library(modelr)
```

broom

When you fit a model, you get an object in return that holds information about the data and the fit. This data is represented in different ways—it depends on the implementation of the function used to fit the data. For a linear model, for example, we get this information:

```
model <- lm(disp ~ hp + wt, data = mtcars)
summary(model)
```

© Thomas Mailund 2019
T. Mailund, *R Data Science Quick Reference*, https://doi.org/10.1007/978-1-4842-4894-2_11

```
##
## Call:
## lm(formula = disp ~ hp + wt, data = mtcars)
##
## Residuals:
##     Min      1Q Median    3Q    Max
## -82.565 -23.802 2.111 35.731 99.107
##
## Coefficients:
##                Estimate Std. Error t value Pr(>|t|)
## (Intercept) -129.9506    29.1890  -4.452 0.000116
## hp             0.6578     0.1649   3.990 0.000411
## wt            82.1125    11.5518   7.108 8.04e-08
##
## (Intercept) ***
## hp          ***
## wt          ***
## ---
## Signif. codes:
## 0 '***' 0.001 '**' 0.01 '*' 0.05 '.' 0.1 ' ' 1
##
## Residual standard error: 47.35 on 29 degrees of freedom
## Multiple R-squared: 0.8635, Adjusted R-squared:   0.8541
## F-statistic: 91.71 on 2 and 29 DF, p-value: 2.889e-13
```

The problem with this representation is that it can be difficult to extract relevant data because the data isn't tidy. The broom package fixes this. It defines three generic function, tidy(), glance(), and augment(). These functions return tibbles. The first gives you the fit, the second a summary of how good the fit is, and the third gives you the original data augmented with fit summaries.

tidy(model) # transform to tidy tibble

```
## # A tibble: 3 x 5
##   term       estimate std.error statistic  p.value
##   <chr>         <dbl>     <dbl>     <dbl>    <dbl>
## 1 (Interce...   -130.      29.2     -4.45  1.16e-4
## 2 hp            0.658     0.165      3.99  4.11e-4
## 3 wt             82.1      11.6      7.11  8.04e-8
```

glance(model) # model summaries

```
## # A tibble: 1 x 11
##   r.squared adj.r.squared sigma statistic   p.value
##       <dbl>         <dbl> <dbl>     <dbl>     <dbl>
## 1     0.863         0.854  47.3      91.7  2.89e-13
## # ...  with 6 more variables: df <int>,
## #  logLik <dbl>, AIC <dbl>, BIC <dbl>,
## #  deviance <dbl>, df.residual <int>
```

augment(model) # add model info to data

```
## # A tibble: 32 x 11
##    .rownames    disp    hp    wt  .fitted  .se.fit
##    <chr>       <dbl> <dbl> <dbl>    <dbl>    <dbl>
##  1 Mazda RX4     160   110  2.62     158.     9.96
##  2 Mazda RX. . . 160   110  2.88     178.     9.53
##  3 Datsun 7. . . 108    93  2.32     122.    11.6
##  4 Hornet 4. . . 258   110  3.22     206.    10.3
##  5 Hornet S. . . 360   175  3.44     268.     9.09
##  6 Valiant       225   105  3.46     223.    12.3
##  7 Duster 3. . . 360   245  3.57     324.    16.2
##  8 Merc 240D     147.   62  3.19     173.    16.1
##  9 Merc 230      141.   95  3.15     191.    11.6
## 10 Merc 280      168.  123  3.44     233.    10.3
```

```
## # . . . with 22 more rows, and 5 more variables:
## #    .resid <dbl>, .hat <dbl>, .sigma <dbl>,
## #    .cooksd <dbl>, .std.resid <dbl>
```

The broom package implements specializations for most models. Not all of the three functions are meaningful for all models, so some models only have a subset of the functions. If you want your own model to work with broom, let us call it mymodel, then you have to implement specializations of the functions, tidy.mymodel(), glance.mymodel(), and augment.mymodel(), that are relevant for the model.

modelr

The modelr package also provides functionality for fitting and inspecting models and for extracting information about model fits. We start with the latter.

Consider the following example model.

```
x <- tibble(
  x = runif(5),
  y = 15 *12 * x + 42 + rnorm(5)
)
model <- lm(y ~ x, data = x)
tidy(model)
```

```
## # A tibble: 2 x 5
##   term       estimate std.error statistic  p.value
##   <chr>         <dbl>     <dbl>     <dbl>    <dbl>
## 1 (Interce. . .  41.8     0.271      154.  5.99e-7
## 2 x             180.      1.15       157.  5.72e-7
```

We have fitted a linear model to data that is sampled from a linear model. The details of the data and model do not matter; it is just an example. I have used the broom function `tidy()` to inspect the model.

Two functions, `add_predictions()` and `add_residuals()`, extend your data with predictions the model would make from each data row and the residuals for each row.

add_predictions(x, model)

```
## # A tibble: 5 x 3
##          x       y   pred
##      <dbl>  <dbl>  <dbl>
## 1 0.445    122.   122.
## 2 0.0594    52.9   52.5
## 3 0.275     91.3   91.4
## 4 0.0311    46.9   47.5
## 5 0.0145    44.7   44.4
```

add_residuals(x, model)

```
## # A tibble: 5 x 3
##          x       y    resid
##      <dbl>  <dbl>   <dbl>
## 1 0.445    122.    0.0653
## 2 0.0594    52.9   0.399
## 3 0.275     91.3  -0.140
## 4 0.0311    46.9  -0.566
## 5 0.0145    44.7   0.242
```

Predictions need not be for existing data. You can create a data frame of explanatory variables and predict the response variable from the new data.

```
xs <- tibble(x = seq(0, 1, length.out = 5))
add_predictions(xs, model)
```

```
## # A tibble: 5 x 2
##        x  pred
##    <dbl> <dbl>
## 1 0       41.8
## 2 0.25    86.9
## 3 0.5    132.
## 4 0.75   177.
## 5 1      222.
```

I know that the x values are in the range from zero to one, but we cannot always a priori know the range that a variable falls within. If you don't know, you can use the seq_range() function to get equidistant points in the range from the lowest to the highest value in your data.

```
seq(0, 1, length.out = 5)
```

```
## [1] 0.00 0.25 0.50 0.75 1.00
```

```
seq_range(x$x, n = 5) # over the range of observations
```

```
## [1] 0.01448234 0.12204440 0.22960645 0.33716850
## [5] 0.44473056
```

If you have two models and want to know how they compare with respect to their predictions, you can use gather_predictions() and spread_predictions():

```
# comparing models
model2 <- lm(y ~ I(x^2) + x, data = x)
gather_predictions(xs, model, model2)
```

```
## # A tibble: 10 x 3
##     model      x  pred
##     <chr>  <dbl> <dbl>
##  1 model      0    41.8
##  2 model   0.25   86.9
##  3 model    0.5  132.
##  4 model   0.75  177.
##  5 model      1  222.
##  6 model2     0    41.9
##  7 model2  0.25   86.8
##  8 model2   0.5  132.
##  9 model2  0.75  178.
## 10 model2     1  223.
```

spread_predictions(xs, model, model2)

```
## # A tibble: 5 x 3
##        x  model model2
##    <dbl>  <dbl>  <dbl>
## 1     0   41.8   41.9
## 2  0.25   86.9   86.8
## 3   0.5  132.   132.
## 4  0.75  177.   178.
## 5     1  222.   223.
```

They show the same data, just with the tables formatted differently. The names gather and spread resembles the tidyr functions gather and spread.

In the previous example, we made predictions on new data, but you can, of course, also do it on your original data.

gather_predictions(x, model,   model2)

```
## # A tibble: 10 x 4
##    model       x        y      pred
##    <chr>    <dbl>    <dbl>    <dbl>
##  1 model    0.445    122.     122.
##  2 model    0.0594    52.9     52.5
##  3 model    0.275     91.3     91.4
##  4 model    0.0311    46.9     47.5
##  5 model    0.0145    44.7     44.4
##  6 model2   0.445    122.     122.
##  7 model2   0.0594    52.9     52.5
##  8 model2   0.275     91.3     91.3
##  9 model2   0.0311    46.9     47.5
## 10 model2   0.0145    44.7     44.5
```

spread_predictions(x, model,   model2)

```
## # A tibble:   5 x 4
##       x        y model model2
##    <dbl>    <dbl> <dbl>  <dbl>
## 1 0.445    122.   122.   122.
## 2 0.0594    52.9   52.5   52.5
## 3 0.275     91.3   91.4   91.3
## 4 0.0311    46.9   47.5   47.5
## 5 0.0145    44.7   44.4   44.5
```

If you have the original data, you can also get residuals.

gather_residuals(x, model, model2)

```
## # A tibble: 10 x 4
##    model        x      y     resid
##    <chr>    <dbl>  <dbl>     <dbl>
##  1 model   0.445   122.    0.0653
##  2 model   0.0594   52.9   0.399
##  3 model   0.275    91.3  -0.140
##  4 model   0.0311   46.9  -0.566
##  5 model   0.0145   44.7   0.242
##  6 model2  0.445   122.    0.0225
##  7 model2  0.0594   52.9   0.412
##  8 model2  0.275    91.3  -0.0710
##  9 model2  0.0311   46.9  -0.578
## 10 model2  0.0145   44.7   0.215
```

spread_residuals(x, model, model2)

```
## # A tibble: 5 x 4
##        x      y    model   model2
##    <dbl>  <dbl>    <dbl>    <dbl>
## 1 0.445   122.    0.0653   0.0225
## 2 0.0594   52.9   0.399    0.412
## 3 0.275    91.3  -0.140   -0.0710
## 4 0.0311   46.9  -0.566   -0.578
## 5 0.0145   44.7   0.242    0.215
```

Depending on the type of data science you usually do, you might have to sample to get empirical distributions or to split your data into training and test data to avoid overfitting. With modelr you have functions for this.

You can build *n* data sets using bootstrapping with the function bootstrap().[1]

bootstrap(x, n = 3)

```
## # A tibble: 3 x 2
##    strap       .id
##    <list>      <chr>
## 1 <resample>  1
## 2 <resample>  2
## 3 <resample>  3
```

It samples random data points and creates *n* new data sets from this. The resulting tibble has two columns: the first, strap, contains the data for each sample and the second an id.

The crossv_mc() function—Monte Carlo cross-validation—creates cross-validation data, that is, it splits your data into training and test data. It creates *n* random data sets divided into test and training data.

crossv_mc(x, n = 3)

```
## # A tibble: 3 x 3
##    train       test        .id
##    <list>      <list>      <chr>
## 1 <resample>  <resample>  1
## 2 <resample>  <resample>  2
## 3 <resample>  <resample>  3
```

By default, the test data is 20% of the sampled data; you can change this using the test argument.

The crossv_kfold and crossv_loo give you k-fold data and leave-one-out data, respectively.

---

[1]There is also a bootstrap() function in broom, but it is deprecated there, so use the modelr function.

crossv_kfold(x, k = 3)

```
## # A tibble: 3 x 3
##   train       test        .id
##   <list>      <list>      <chr>
## 1 <resample>  <resample>  1
## 2 <resample>  <resample>  2
## 3 <resample>  <resample>  3
```

crossv_loo(x)

```
## # A tibble: 5 x 3
##   train       test         .id
##   <list>      <list>       <int>
## 1 <resample>  <resample>      1
## 2 <resample>  <resample>      2
## 3 <resample>  <resample>      3
## 4 <resample>  <resample>      4
## 5 <resample>  <resample>      5
```

As an example, say you have sampled three bootstrap data sets. The samples are in the strap column, so we can map over it and fit a linear model to each sampled data set.

```
samples <- bootstrap(x, 3)
fitted_models <- samples$strap %>%
  map(~ lm(y ~ x, data = .))
```

Then we can map over the three models and inspect them using broom's glance() function:

```
fitted_models %>%
  map(glance) %>%
  bind_rows()
```

```
## # A tibble: 3 x 11
##    r.squared adj.r.squared sigma statistic  p.value
##        <dbl>         <dbl> <dbl>     <dbl>    <dbl>
## 1     1.000         1.000 0.171   160710.  3.42e-8
## 2     1.000         1.000 0.513    16835.  1.01e-6
## 3     1.000         1.000 0.485    17065.  9.89e-7
## # . . . with 6 more variables: df <int>,
## #   logLik <dbl>, AIC <dbl>, BIC <dbl>,
## #   deviance <dbl>, df.residual <int>
```

If we were interested in the empirical distribution of x, then we could extract the distribution over the bootstrapped data and go from there.

```
get_x <- function(m) {
  tidy(m) %>% filter(term == "x") %>%
    select(estimate) %>% as.double()
}
fitted_models %>% map_dbl(get_x)
```

```
## [1] 179.3946 180.6586 180.0705
```

If you want to compare models, rather than samples of your data, then modelr has support for that as well. You can make a list of the formulae you want to fit. The formulae() function lets you create such a list.

```
models <- formulae(~y, linear = ~x, quadratic = ~I(x^2) + x)
```

The first argument is the response variable (the left-hand side of the formulae), and the remaining arguments are (named) parameters that describe the explanatory variables, the righthand part of a model formula.

If you call fit_with() with your data, the fitting function to use (here lm()) and the formulae you wish to fit, then you get what you want—a fit for each formula.

```
fits <- fit_with(x, lm, models)
fits %>% map(glance) %>% bind_rows()

## # A tibble: 2 x 11
##   r.squared adj.r.squared sigma statistic  p.value
##       <dbl>         <dbl> <dbl>     <dbl>    <dbl>
## 1     1.000         1.000 0.433    24589.  5.72e-7
## 2     1.000         1.000 0.527     8310.  1.20e-4
## # . . . with 6 more variables: df <int>,
## # logLik <dbl>, AIC <dbl>, BIC <dbl>,
## # deviance <dbl>, df.residual <int>
```

You will find many model quality measures in modelr. For example, root-mean-square error

```
fits %>% map_dbl(rmse, data = x)

##    linear quadratic
## 0.3354516 0.3331588
```

mean-absolute-error

```
fits %>% map_dbl(mae, data = x)

##    linear quadratic
## 0.2826265 0.2595208
```

and many more.

Since overfitting is always a problem, you might want to use a quality measure that, at least attemps to, take model complexity into account. You have some in the glance() function from broom.

```
fits %>% map_dbl(~ glance(.x)$AIC)

##    linear quadratic
## 9.266611 11.198024
```

If at all possible, however, you want to use test data to measure how well a model generalizes. For this, you first need to fit your models to the training data and then make predictions on the test data. In the following example, I have fitted lm(y ~ x) on leave-one-out data and then applied it on the test data. I then measure the quality of the generalization using RMSE.

```
samples <- crossv_loo(x)
training_fits <-
  samples$train %>% map(~lm(y ~ x, data = .))
test_measurement <- training_fits %>%
  map2_dbl(samples$test, rmse)

test_measurement

##         1         2         3         4         5
## 0.2618250 0.5535395 0.1963251 0.8401988 0.3776097
```

Plotting: `ggplot2`

The `ggplot2` package contains a vast number of functions for creating a wide variety of plots. It would take an entire book to cover it all—there are already several that cover it—so I cannot attempt this here. In this chapter, I will only try to give you a flavor of how the package works.

The `ggplot2` package is loaded when you load `tidyverse`, but you can always include it on its own using

```
library(ggplot2)
```

The Basic Plotting Components in `ggplot2`

Unlike in R's base graphics, with `ggplot2` you do not create individual plot components by drawing lines, points, or whatever you need onto a graphics canvas. Instead, you specify how your data should be mapped to abstract graphical aesthetics, for example, x- and y-coordinates, colors, shapes, and so on. Then you specify how aesthetics should be represented in the graphics, for example, whether x- and y-coordinates should be plotted as scatter plots or lines. On top of this can add graphics information such as which shapes points in a scatter plot should have, which colors the color aesthetics maps, and such. You add attributes as separate steps which makes it easy to change a plot. If you want to add a linear regression to your plot, you can do it with a single command; since `ggplot2` already knows which of your data variables are mapped to the x- and y-coordinates, it simply computes the linear regression and adds it

© Thomas Mailund 2019
T. Mailund, *R Data Science Quick Reference*, https://doi.org/10.1007/978-1-4842-4894-2_12

to the plot. If you want to plot your data on a log scale, you tell `ggplot2` that the axis should be log-transformed.

At first, `ggplot2` might seem more complicated than basic R's graphics, but you will soon get used to it.

The main components of `ggplot2` are these:

- Data—Obviously, you have data you want to plot.

- Aesthetics—Aesthetics map data to abstract graphical concepts such as x- and y-coordinates, colors and fills.

- Geometries—Geometries, geometric objects, determine which kind of plot you are making, for example, whether you will get a histogram, a scatter plot, or a boxplot.

- Statistics—How should the data be summarized before plotting. Your data is not always summarized, that is, the statistics can be the identity mapping. A scatter plot doesn't compute a summary for the x- and y-coordinates, but a regression line or a histogram does.

- Scales—Scales specify how the data you mapped to graphical concepts with the aesthetics should actually be placed on a plot. Your x- and y-coordinate data might be measured in meters, but those meters should be mapped to points on your plot. The scales are responsible for this.

- Coordinates—Coordinates allow you to transform the result of scaling your data to plot components. If, for example, you want your plot to show the y-axis on a log scale, then the coordinates transformation does this.

- Faceting—Faceting splits your plot into subplots based on the variables in your data.

You create a ggplot2 plot using the ggplot() function. To that object, you add one or more of the preceding components. Nothing happens until you print the graphical object; printing it will make the plot. A typical pattern is to plot it right away and add the components in the same statement in which you create the graphical object.

ggplot(. . .) + . . . components . . .

To add components to a plot, you use *addition*. The ggplot2 package does *not* use pipelines. You often see data piped into the ggplot() call, though, but after that, you must remember to add rather than pipe.

A *layer* creates (part of) the graphics you can see. At a minimum, it must consist of data, aesthetics, statistics (can be the identity), and a geometric object (that might specify the statistics). Your plot must have at least one layer before your plot shows your data.

Adding Components to Plot Objects

The simplest plot we can create is empty. You can create it by calling ggplot() without any arguments.

p <- **ggplot**()

You can see what it consists of by calling the summary() function, but most of the information is not relevant here. I will highlight lines relevant to the components we see in this section as we go along.

summary(p)

```
## data: [x]
## faceting: <ggproto object: Class FacetNull, Facet, gg>
##      compute_layout: function
##      draw_back: function
##      draw_front: function
```

```
##      draw_labels: function
##      draw_panels: function
##      finish_data: function
##      init_scales: function
##      map_data: function
##      params: list
##      setup_data: function
##      setup_params: function
##      shrink: TRUE
##      train_scales: function
##      vars: function
##    super: <ggproto object: Class FacetNull, Facet, gg>
```

To create a plot, you print the plot object. You can do this explicitly

print(p)

or just type it into your R terminal.

p

Since putting an object at the outermost level in an R script will print an object, ggplot objects are not always assigned to a variable and then plotted later. You can just write the ggplot() object.

ggplot()

Why would anyone create an empty plot object? You cannot print the empty object. Well, you can, but you will get an empty canvas, so there is not much point to that. You can, however, build up a plot by adding components to it. You can start with the empty plot and add all you want to it in separate commands.

Adding Data

You add data to a plot as an argument to ggplot(). If you want to add data to the empty plot, you will use geometries; see the following example. If you add data in the ggplot() function, then all components you add to the plot later will be able to see the data.

With some random test data, we can create a plot object with associated data.

```
dat <- tibble(
  foo = runif(100),
  bar = 20 * foo + 5 + rnorm(100, sd = 10),
  baz = rep(1:2, each = 50)
)
p <- ggplot(data = dat)
```

If you call summary(p) you can see the line:

```
data: foo, bar, baz [100x3]
```

It shows you the variables in the data. They are not mapped to any graphical objects yet; that is the purview of aesthetics.

Adding Aesthetics

What we see in a plot are points, lines, colors, and so on. To create these plots, ggplot2 needs to know which variables in the data should be interpreted as coordinates, which determines line thickness, which determines colors and so on. Aesthetics do this.

Consider this plot object:

```
p <- ggplot(data = dat, aes(x = foo, y = bar, color = baz))
```

Here, we have specified that foo determines the x-coordinate, bar the y-coordinate, and baz the color. If you check the summary of the plot, you can see the mapping from data variables to graphical objects below the data line:

```
data: foo, bar, baz [100x3]
mapping:  x = ~foo, y = ~bar, colour = ~baz
```

Plotting (printing) this will give you an empty plot where the x- and y-axes match the range of the data's x and y (foo and bar) values. The plot is otherwise empty because it does not have a geometry.

Adding Geometries

Geometries specify the type of the plot. They use the aesthetics' maps from the data to graphical properties and create a plot based on them.

One of the most straightforward plots is a scatter plot. We can add the geom_point() geometry to the plot we created previously to get a scatter plot.

```
p <- ggplot(data = dat, aes(x = foo, y = bar, color = baz)) +
    geom_point()
```

If you call summary(p), you will see these lines at the bottom of the output:

```
geom_point: na.rm = FALSE
stat_identity: na.rm = FALSE
```

They tell you that you have a point geometry and that the statistic that maps from the data to a summary is the identity. We do not make any summary of the data when we plot it as points. You can create the plot by printing the plot object; you can see the result in Figure 12-1.

```
print(p)
```

You can add data and aesthetics directly to the geometry. This is especially useful if you want to overlay alternative data onto a plot but as an example consider moving the same data and aesthetics to the geom_ point() call.

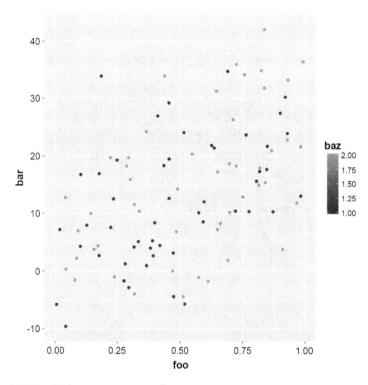

Figure 12-1. *Point geometry plot*

```
p <- ggplot() +
  geom_point(data = dat, aes(x = foo, y = bar, color = baz))
```

If you look at the summary, you will see that the mapping from the aesthetics is now grouped with the geometry

```
mapping: x = ~foo, y = ~bar, colour = ~baz
geom_point: na.rm = FALSE
stat_identity: na.rm = FALSE
```

but otherwise, there is little change. This can be used to add additional data to a plot. It also shows that it sometimes can make sense to start with an empty plot object and then add different data sets in different geometries.

Since baz is numerical, it is interpreted as a continuous variable. You can get a discrete color mapping by transforming it into a factor.

```
ggplot(data = dat, aes(x = foo, y = bar, color = factor(baz)))
+ geom_point()
```

You can see the result in Figure 12-2.

You can change the levels in the factor to reorder the legend. See Chapter 9 for more on manipulating factors.

Another simple geometry is a line plot.

```
ggplot(data = arrange(dat, foo),
       aes(x = foo, y = bar, color = factor(baz))) +
  geom_line()
```

Figure 12-2. *Discrete color aesthetics*

Figure 12-3. *A line plot*

See the result in Figure 12-3. I sorted the data with respect to the x-axis before I plotted it using arrange(). Otherwise, the lines would not go left to right.

You can have more than one geometry, for example:

```
p <- ggplot(data = dat, aes(x = foo, y = bar, color = baz)) +
          geom_point() + geom_smooth(method = "loess")
```

If you call summary(p), you will see two layers at the bottom of the output.

```
geom_point: na.rm = FALSE
stat_identity: na.rm = FALSE
position_identity
```

```
geom_smooth: na.rm = FALSE, se = TRUE
stat_smooth: na.rm = FALSE, se = TRUE, # more here. . .
position_identity
```

Observe that the smooth geometry does not have the identity statistics. It shows a summary of the data and the mapping from the data to that summary is handled by a stat_smooth statistics.

We can print the plot

print(p)

Figure 12-4. *Plot with two geometries*

and see the result in Figure 12-4.

If we use a discrete color, it also groups the data, so if we make baz a factor again, we will get the data in a differently colored point and get two smoothed lines.

ggplot(data = dat, **aes**(x = foo, y = bar, color = **factor**(baz))) +
  geom_point() + **geom_smooth**(method = "loess")

See the result in Figure 12-5.

You can build a histogram plot with geom_histogram() (see Figure 12-6).

ggplot(data = dat, **aes**(x = foo)) + **geom_histogram**(binwidth = 0.05)

Notice that you only need an x-axis for this geometry. With summary(p) you will see that the statistic is stat_bin.

```
geom_bar: na.rm = FALSE
stat_bin: binwidth = NULL, # there is more here
```

If you want a density plot instead, you use geom_density().

ggplot(data = dat, **aes**(x = bar)) + **geom_density**()

There, you will see that the statistic is stat_density.

```
geom_density: na.rm = FALSE
```

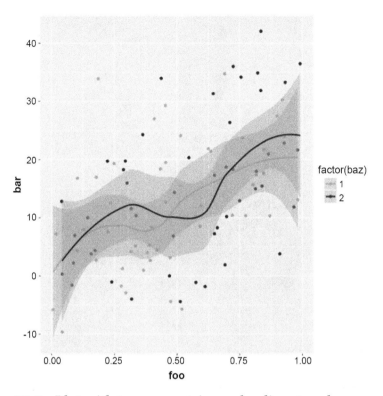

Figure 12-5. *Plot with two geometries and a discrete color*

Figure 12-6. *Histogram plot*

stat_density: na.rm = FALSE

I think you see the pattern now.

Facets

The effect of adding a grid facet is that we get sub-figures where the data is split into groups determined by the formula we give facet_grid(); see Figure 12-7.

ggplot(data = dat, **aes**(x = foo, y = bar)) + **geom_point**() +
  facet_grid(~ **factor**(baz))

In the previous plots, when you looked at their summary, you would see, under `faceting`, that the class was `FacetNull`.

```
faceting: <ggproto object: Class FacetNull, Facet, gg>
```

When we added the grid facet, we now see this:

```
faceting: <ggproto object: Class FacetGrid, Facet, gg>
```

You can plot in a two-dimensional grid by having variables on both sides of the formula:

```
dat2 <- tibble(
  foo = rep(1:5, each = 20),
  bar = rep(1:2, each = 50),
  x = foo * bar + rnorm(100),
  y = -foo
)
ggplot(data = dat2, aes(x = x, y = y)) +
  geom_point() + facet_grid(factor(foo) ~ factor(bar))
```

Figure 12-7. *Faceting the plot*

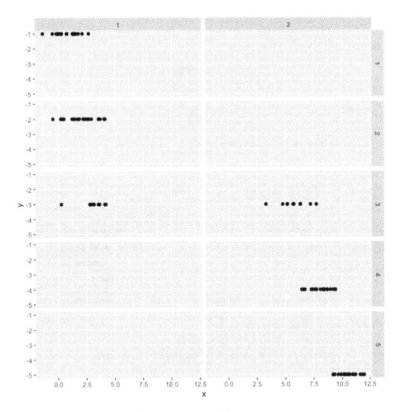

Figure 12-8. *Facet grid for two variables*

The result is shown in Figure 12-8.

You can use more than two variables but (naturally) only two dimensions. If you use more than two variables, then the different categories will be shown as labels on the facet sides. You will see all combinations of factors that appear in the formula. As an example, consider this:

```
dat3 <- tibble(
  foo = factor(rep(1:5, each = 20)),
  bar = factor(rep(1:2, each = 50)),
  baz = factor(rep(1:5, times = 20)),
  qux = factor(rep(1:2, times = 50)),
```

```
  x = rnorm(100),
  y = rnorm(100)
)
ggplot(data = dat3, aes(x = x, y = y)) +
  geom_point() + facet_grid(foo + bar ~ baz + qux)
```

The result is shown in Figure 12-9.

Adding Coordinates

All the preceding plots were plotted in cartesian coordinates—the default coordinates. You can change the coordinates of a plot. For example, you can flip an axis, for example, the x-axis of a plot:

```
ggplot(data = dat, aes(x = foo, y = bar)) + geom_point() +
coord_flip()
```

Or you can plot in polar coordinates instead of cartesian coordinates.

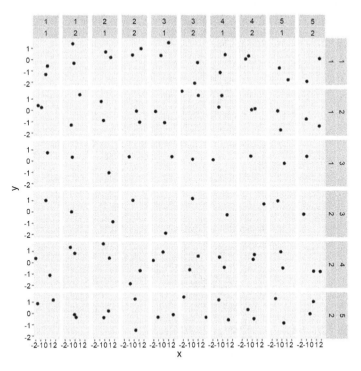

Figure 12-9. *Facet with four variables*

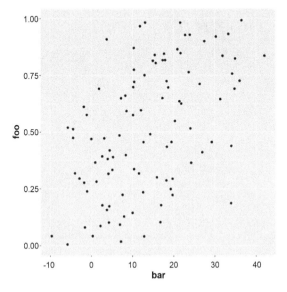

Figure 12-10. *Plot with the x-coordinate flipped*

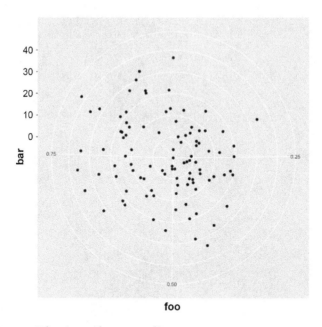

Figure 12-11. *Plot in polar coordinates*

ggplot(data = dat, **aes**(x = foo, y = bar)) + **geom_point**() +
  coord_polar()

See Figures 12-10 and 12-11.

CHAPTER 13

Conclusions

R, extended with the Tidyverse, is a powerful language for data science. There is strong support for each step along a data analysis pipeline. After reading this book, you should have a good grasp of how the Tidyverse packages work and how you use them. The book did not cover which data science and machine learning model to use on particular data, but only how they could fit into pipelines. Covering actual data analysis and the methods to use—and packages supporting them—is beyond the scope of this book. Each statistical or machine learning method could fill a book in itself, and there are many such models in R packages. The book is mainly a syntax guide and what it covered can be used with any model you need to apply to your data, so it is a good foundation for how to adapt your data analysis into the Tidyverse framework.

© Thomas Mailund 2019
T. Mailund, *R Data Science Quick Reference*, https://doi.org/10.1007/978-1-4842-4894-2_13

Index

A

arrange() function, 125, 228

B

bootstrap() function, 214
boundary() function, 165
broom package
    augment(), 207
    example, 205
    glance() function, 207, 215
    tidy(), 206

C

col_factor(), 19, 21
col_ functions, 20
Column encodings
    convert argument, 52
    extract() function, 54
    remove argument, 52, 56
    separate() function, 51, 52
    separate_rows(), 56, 57
Column types
    function-based
        specification, 18–22
    string-based (*see* String-based
        specification)

complete() function, 60, 61
crossing() function, 59

D

Data frame
    column selection
        contains() function, 115
        ends_with() function,
          113–115
        indices, 111, 112
        matches() function, 115
        non-empty strings, 116
        ranges, 112
        rename, 117
        select(), 110, 117
        sorting, 125, 126
        starts_with() function, 113
    example, countries income
        dplyr, 155
        mean_income, 158
        missing data, 155
        mutate(), 157
        reformatting, 156, 157
        ungroup table, 159
Data frames modification
    abs() function, 131
    add columns, 128

© Thomas Mailund 2019
T. Mailund, *R Data Science Quick Reference*, https://doi.org/10.1007/978-1-4842-4894-2